MW01533818

# God, Sherryl and Me

## A Romantic Story of Miracles, Love and Second Chances

## Gordon Allen Perkins

Xulon Press
11350 Random Hills Road
Suite 800
Fairfax, VA 22030
(703) 279-6511
XulonPress.com

To order additional copies, call 1-866-909-BOOK (2665).

# Table of Contents

# Chapter One

# I Remember the Beginning

***

$\mathcal{A}$re certain people destined to be together? Is there such a thing as soul mates? I don't know. I suppose I would probably say no. But in my life circumstances seem to point to a guiding hand that eventually brought my wife Sherryl and me together. Everything hasn't turned out perfectly. The life we have shared has had its struggles, but it has also been a wonderful adventure. We have experienced miracles. That's right, miracles, several of them. Some were big and some were small. If this story ever gets published, it may qualify as the next one.

I am writing this book because God is compelling me to. I started to write our story years ago, but something halted that effort. I think it was because it just wasn't time yet. There have been some major struggles we have had to face in the last few years. We have learned a lot about ourselves and about the Lord as we've faced these recent challenges.

This book chronicles how God has watched over Sherryl and me. We didn't do anything to deserve it. God's grace is simply a gift. What we have done is recognize His grace and intercession on our behalf. I could title this book **God Takes Care of Idiots.** We really feel that way, when Sherryl and I think about all the bad decisions we have made, and all the times we have disappointed the Lord. In spite of that, God has blessed us with miracles. We do what we can to serve Him simply because we are grateful.

It's funny how certain events are stamped on our memories. Things that others forget or view as unimportant can be imprinted on our minds, there for reasons we never understand until years later. Do you have memories like that? Ones that go way back to your childhood. Memories that shouldn't be that important but for some reason have always stayed fresh. I have a few. For example, I remember an incident that happened when I was three years old. My family lived in an older home in the village of Wellington, Ohio. My parents had just finished building a new home two miles west of town, next to a small bowling alley they owned and operated. We were in the process of moving and I was in our old house watching this wasp circle around the ceiling. I alerted one of my older siblings to the clear and present danger. I was the youngest of four children. My oldest sister Gayle was eleven years older than me, Glenda was eight years older and my brother Gary was six years older. I don't remember which one of them did it, but one of them riled that wasp up in an effort to get it out of the house, and injustice of all injustice, the wasp came down and stung **me.** Nobody else remembers that event, but I have never forgotten it, even though I was only three years old. I suppose that is understandable since I was the person stung.

Another one of those memories focused on my first encounter with Sherryl. Little did I know when it occurred, that Sherryl would become a very important person in my life. Sherryl doesn't remember our first meeting at all. Neither does her father, but it has always been one of those special memories of mine, and I think I even know why.

It was late May, just a few days before school was finished for the year. Sherryl must have been about six years old. I was about ten and playing baseball on a team her father coached. The team practiced on a ball field behind the Brighton School.

Brighton School was the alma mater of both my mother and father and Sherryl's dad as well. The school system had been consolidated into the Wellington School System several years before, but the building was still being used for grades one through eight for the children who lived in Brighton Township. Even though my home was less than a mile from Sherryl's, we didn't go to the same school. I went to Wellington and she went to Brighton, so I didn't know her.

One spring day after my baseball practice was over, this cute little blonde girl started chasing me all around the baseball field. The image of her running after me carrying her lunch box, for some reason, always stayed with me. I finally tired and the little girl caught up to me. Suddenly, **"POW"** she belted me right in the head with her metal lunch box. I wasn't bleeding, but it did hurt. She looked like she had every intention of doing it again, so I ran over to the coach for protection. I told him about the girl clobbering me with her lunch box, and that's when I learned that she was his daughter.

I never forgot what her dad said when I told him what his daughter had done to me. "She hit you because she likes you," he said.

I also never forgot what I said back to him. "I'd hate to see what she'd do to me if she loved me," I complained. Little did I know at the time, one day I would find that out. When I did, I wouldn't complain.

Believe it or not, I have always known why I remembered

that first meeting with Sherryl. It was because that was the first time in my life that a person of the opposite sex seemed to show an interest in me. Even though she was a little pest, I was flattered. All my early attempts to get girls to notice me seemed like complete failures. In first grade, I liked this girl named Jenny. She never seemed to acknowledge I existed, so I decided girls just weren't worth the effort. Even though it hurt, Sherryl's effort to get me to notice her was a pleasant surprise, a lift to a fragile male ego.

It would be more than two decades and a failed marriage for both of us, but friendship and then love would bring Sherryl and me together again. Her lunch box literally made the first impression on me. Her pure heart and caring nature made the next impression, over twenty years later.

# Chapter Two

# Between Meetings

High School days were wonderful for both Sherryl and me. We never knew each other during our high school years because of the difference in our ages. When I was a senior, Sherryl was only in the eighth grade.

I won eight varsity letters in high school playing football, basketball and baseball. I loved sports and I was fairly successful in everything I tried. I got good grades and was a class officer. I made National Honor Society as a senior. I was a relatively big fish in the small pond that was Wellington High School.

My high school days were some of the happiest times in my life. I had four very good friends who I had grown up playing sports with. We called ourselves the "Big Five." We were all good students and good athletes. We were pretty popular as well. Between us, we had representation in most of the areas of responsibility in school. We were class officers, student council members, and various club leaders. We were all involved and enjoyed those years immensely.

When I was in the sixth grade I chipped my front two teeth. My teeth were not my best asset before this happened. They were big, far from perfect, and I had an overbite. Get the picture? I kind of had buck teeth. Now, it was even worse, because an inverted V-notch existed in these front teeth from being chipped. For some reason, I never had these teeth capped until midway through my senior year. Because I was so self conscious about my teeth, I was reluctant to ever smile with my mouth open. In the years since school, I learned that some of my classmates thought I was stuck up because I seldom smiled. Little did they know how embarrassed I was about my teeth. Those teeth probably had a lot to do with my not having any serious girl friends in high school as well.

When I began my freshman year of college, Sherryl began her freshman year at Wellington High School. Sherryl was a cheerleader, homecoming queen, and student counsel representative. She was involved in many school activities and was very popular. She was a better student than I was and was selected to National Honor Society as a junior. Today she has many problems with her memory but she never has had a problem remembering that I wasn't selected for NHS until I was a senior.

Sherryl didn't have any physical appearance flaws like my chipped teeth either. Physically she was a knockout. She is a social animal and always has been. In grade school she often got into trouble and had to sit in the hall for being a "walker and a talker." She is and always has been friendly and talkative. Even so, socially she didn't always fit in. Her strong church upbringing made many of the things others were doing unacceptable to her.

Sherryl didn't have any serious boyfriends during high school by her choice. She was good friends with many of the boys. She tells me boys were easier to be friends with because girls were often very petty. I'm sure the boys wanted to be friends with her. Sherryl wanted to be friends with all the girls too, but often girls make that a very hard thing to do.

In many ways Sherryl and I had similar high school experiences. We were both very active, athletic, popular and good students. Sherryl describes herself as being a "goody goodie two shoes." In many ways, so was I.

I graduated from high school in 1966. It is strange how it seems like only a short time ago. I have learned something interesting about how the human mind works. Pleasant memories seem to linger in perpetual freshness. Unpleasant times seem to simply disappear. They can only be recalled through focused effort. It is a wonderful tendency that God seems to have built into us.

The Vietnam War was just heating up at that time. I was accepted at Bowling Green State University. I loved playing football but I thought I might have a chance to play baseball professionally. I didn't have a scholarship to Bowling Green, but I was recruited by the baseball coach there. I decided to go to Bowling Green because I thought it was my best path to a professional baseball career. One of my close friends and a member of the "Big Five," Dave, was going to be my roommate. He was going out for the baseball team too.

About a month before college was going to start, I was contacted by Lee Tressel. Mr. Tressel was the head football coach at Baldwin Wallace College. He said he really wanted me to attend BW and there I could play both football and baseball. Football was my favorite sport and I was pretty good at it. I played split end and defensive back in high school. I had been very interested in BW during my senior year as a possible choice for college. I even went to four of their home football games to watch them play. That was the problem. They almost never threw a pass. I wanted to catch passes. It is hard to catch passes when you never throw them.

Coach Tressel told me he was changing his offense to one

that would feature the pass. He said I was exactly the type of player he was looking for. The problem was I didn't believe him. I couldn't convince myself that a football coach would really change his style so dramatically.

In my life the two decisions I regret the most, are two I made when I failed to listen to my father. Going to Bowling Green was the first one. Dad wanted me to go to Baldwin Wallace even though it would be more expensive. He thought I would get a better education and enjoy playing both football and baseball. He was right, but I didn't listen. I turned down a small grant from BW based on my parent's financial need.

Instead I went to Bowling Green State University and I learned a valuable lesson. I didn't have good discernment. The varsity baseball coach at Bowling Green was very nice to Dave and I. He told us both how good we were and how much he wanted us to come to BGSU. He told us Bowling Green didn't give out baseball scholarships to freshmen, but if we made the freshmen team, scholarships were available after that. I found out after I started school, the coach had lied to us. There were several freshmen players that had received athletic scholarships.

In the fall of my freshman year at Bowling Green, I went out for the baseball team. Even though I had won four varsity letters as a second baseman in high school, I went to BG and said I was a third baseman. I was shocked to learn there were sixty-four infielders trying to make the freshman team. I was one of sixteen third basemen. That first day of practice they told us that after three days they were going to cut that number down from sixty-four to twelve, three for each infield position.

I played the best baseball of my life. I never bobbled a ground ball, and I hit the ball with authority. After the third day, I learned that I had made that first cut. Unfortunately Dave didn't.

I continued to play well, and when the season began in the spring, I was the starting third baseman. The freshman baseball team only had a twelve game schedule. I started the first six games and the team was undefeated. I was 12 for 21, a batting average of .572, the highest on the team. I hadn't made an error and my dreams of playing professionally were looking like they could come true. Then I was benched.

The varsity baseball coach told the freshman coach to bench me and play another player whose father was an alumni. The boy's father had been driving up from Cincinnati to watch his son play and he was upset because he wasn't starting. I didn't get in to even pitch hit for the next five games. I started the final game at Ohio State and that ended the season.

When I went to meet with the varsity baseball coach about receiving scholarship money for next year, he said all the scholarships were gone. He said since I had split time with the other player he wasn't sure how much I would play for the varsity. I left his office and went out and did some checking with other freshmen players. I learned that six players that never started a game received some scholarship money.

I went back to meet with the varsity coach. I told him I was sick and tired of all his lies and that I was going to transfer to Baldwin Wallace College. I will never forget what he said to me. "If you do that, you'll be an athletic bum."

I stood up, tears welling in my eyes and leaned over his desk. "There's only one bum in this room," I said, "and I'm looking at him."

I tell this story because of the lesson I should have learned from it. Discernment is something we all need. I was flattered by the attention the varsity baseball coach at Bowling Green had paid to me, while he was trying to recruit me. I was impressed by the size of the school and the facilities. The coach told me many things that were not true. He lied and he was good at it. He could look you right in the eye and it didn't bother him at all to lie. I guess the ends justified the means in his mind.

Many people assume that what they are being told is true. We often believe lies because we don't take the time to check out the integrity or the motives of the source we are depending on. Some extra effort on my part would have made me realize that the baseball coach at Bowling Green was not to be trusted. That same extra effort could have made me understand that Coach Tressel at Baldwin Wallace could be trusted.

I have had sources who were supposed to be authoritative tell me things that turned out to be untrue. Sometimes the untruths were simply mistakes, sometimes they were intentional misinformation. The point is, we have to find a way to discern who and what we can believe. I have come to realize that the Bible is my starting point for discernment. Now, if what I hear goes against Biblical standards or principles, the issue is settled for me. I did not discern the character of the Bowling Green varsity baseball coach correctly. I did not discern the character of my first wife correctly either. Sherryl's discernment regarding her first husband also proved to be wrong. We can be fooled and sometimes we want to fool ourselves.

Do you know why magicians can appear to do impossible illusions? The reason they can succeed in fooling us is because we want to be fooled. Often a magician lies to the audience or uses a prearranged helper that he denies ever knowing, in order to pull off an amazing trick. Because we want to be fooled, we assume the magician would never lie. Guess what, they use that tendency in us to their advantage. So does the devil. Many people don't want to know the truth and Satan knows it. He uses that to deceive us. He's deceived us so well today that many people, who think they are very intelligent, don't even believe that truth exists.

Discernment, it is an essential thing to have. Ask God to help you develop it and use his word to cultivate it.

Like I said before, Sherryl and I were both "goody goodie two shoes" in high school. I never got into smoking or drinking or using bad language. Sometimes my friends would kid me because I would tell them to stop swearing. The same was true with Sherryl, but to an even greater extent. She was pretty straight laced because of her strong church upbringing. Her parents didn't let her go on a date before she was sixteen. In my case, it wasn't really the influence of the church, because we didn't go to church much. It was just the way my parents were at home. Sherryl and I were both pretty compliant children.

When I went to Bowling Green I didn't change dramatically, but I did occasionally go have some beers with the guys. I even smoked a few cigarettes trying to stay awake studying. The only night at college I ever really over did it was the last night before final exams were over my freshman year.

I had the meeting with the varsity baseball coach a few days earlier and he made me grow to hate Bowling Green State University. As far as I was concerned, he was a liar and an arrogant hypocrite. He had been so nice while recruiting me, and treated me unfairly once I was there. He lied about scholarships and didn't keep his word. Looking back on it, maybe it was all for the best and just part of God's plan. I don't like what he did to me, but I do forgive him. I have to because God commands it. Still I can't help but wonder what would have happened if he had kept his word.

My freshman year at Bowling Green I was housed on the top floor of Rogers Dorm with most of the other freshman athletes. The last night before the final day of school almost everyone on the dorm floor went downtown to celebrate. Eventually I ended up downtown too, at the most popular watering hole, "The Canterbury Inn." I sat with about fifteen members of the freshman baseball team. They had put several tables together to make one long table. Several of the guys had been there quite a while before I arrived. One of them, Mickey, a back up catcher, never did anything in moderation. If you ever saw the movie "Animal House," Mickey would have fit right into that fraternity. By the time I arrived Mickey was already three sheets into the wind. He was tanked! The place was packed and everyone was celebrating the year coming to an end. Before I finished my first beer, Mickey had laid his face down on the table, and seemed to have passed out. Every once in a while he would groan or move a little, just enough to let the rest of us know that he was still alive. We were all seated around the table reminiscing over the baseball season that had just ended, when suddenly Mickey stirred and sat up. He mumbled a few words no one could understand, then he moved his chair and turned around and laid his head down on a small round table for two behind us. There was a guy and his date seated at the table. They just laughed understandingly and moved their drinks over a little and kindly tolerated Mickey's intrusion into their space. The rest of us laughed with them and since Mickey seemed to be OK, we all went back to our conversations. About a minute later we heard a scream and some loud curse words. Mickey had vomited all over the couple's table.

Suddenly there was a big commotion. Several bouncers for the place (all of them football players) came over and were preparing to throw Mickey out. Personally, I thought it was a pretty good idea, but the other freshman baseball players took it as an attack on the whole team. Some of them stood up and argued Mickey's case. The bouncers decided to let Mickey stay, as other workers cleaned the area up. The biggest bouncer of them all left us with his stern warning, "All right, he can stay, but you guys watch him. If he throws up again or causes any trouble, you're all out of here!"

The team accepted the bouncer's terms. Mickey stayed.

Now back at our table, it wasn't long before he had his head down sleeping again. We all quickly forgot about him and continued socializing. A few minutes later, Mickey slid down off his chair and laid on the floor under our table. Boy, was he sloshed, but he looked comfortable enough so we let him stay down there.

Mickey laid on the floor under our table sleeping for about half an hour. Everyone just forgot about him. Then came the SCREAM! I mean we all heard a first class scream coming from a girl at a table just a few feet from us. Mickey had crawled out from under our table and slithered unnoticed beneath hers. He decided to conduct his own private panty raid right there. The next thing I knew, total chaos broke out. A gang of bouncers came storming over. The freshman baseball players were saying you can't throw one of us out. They were right, they threw us all out. There was a giant hand on my shirt collar and another one giving me a terrible wedgie as it lifted up the back of my jeans. The next thing I remember was rolling on the sidewalk outside the front doors of the establishment. Once I gathered my senses, I felt lucky not to be in jail.

I tell this story because that stupid night of folly had a long lasting affect on my life. Because of my drinking that night, I missed a final exam I had for a history course the next day. That brought my grade point average down to one tenth of a point below what I needed to transfer to Baldwin Wallace College. That meant I had to return to Bowling Green for the first semester of my sophomore year to raise my grade point average. When you transfer schools, you loose one year of athletic eligibility. It kept me from ever playing college football, because I was only eligible my senior year.

I transferred to Baldwin Wallace in the middle of my sophomore year. I did play two years of varsity baseball there, but I always regretted not playing football. Once I got to BW, I really got to know coach Lee Tressel. I should have believed him when he said he was going to a passing offense and I would enjoy playing for him. He didn't lie. BW has been passing ever since. Coach Tressel's son Dick played on the baseball team with me. Lee Tressel's legacy as a great football coach lives on in his sons. Dick went on to be a head coach at a division three college. He joined his younger brother, Jim Tressel, who won division 1A national championships as head coach at Youngstown State and who is now the head football coach at The Ohio State University.

I didn't listen to my father on my choice of college and I regret it. The other decision I made that I regret was my choice of who I married in 1969. Both my Dad and my brother Gary tried to warn me. Dad saw problems in our relationship and recognized some character traits in my girl that I chose to ignore. Gary's evaluation was a little more superficial. "Her thighs are too big," Gary warned.

Dad's concerns had substance. Gary's seemed important to him but not to me. They were seeing things with some objectivity. I wasn't. I couldn't because in addition to not listening to my Dad, I wasn't listening to my heavenly Father's advice either.

My brother Gary was six years older than me. He graduated from Ohio University in 1964. He was a Captain in the Army and a helicopter pilot. Gary was much more of a party animal than I was. A good athlete and student, he was married and had two small children when he was killed in Vietnam in 1968. He was twenty-six years old. Gary was a free spirit and everyone liked him. He had a promising career ahead of him in the Army. Gary was awarded the Distinguished Flying Cross for his heroism. His death changed my draft status to that of a sole surviving son. His sacrifice insulated me from the Vietnam War. I never served in the military, but I deeply respect all who do. There is no greater love than the love of one who will give his life for another. I hope Gary knew the Lord and I will see him again one day.

I was blessed with wonderful parents. They were very supportive. They always attended all the kids activities. I can't remember them ever missing one of my games. I was a pretty compliant child. Even so, I know that some of my activities weren't that easy to put up with.

Midway through my senior year of high school, music started being a bigger part of my life. The Beatles were huge then, and what they did suddenly looked like it would be fun to me. Sports were still king, but music now had my attention.

A friend from the high school football team was a lead guitar player. We got the bright idea of putting a band together. He taught me how to play the bass guitar. My cousin Mike played the electric organ. The drummer and lead singer were other friends from high school who were both juniors. We met and practiced for several weeks. We saved our money and bought equipment. "The Bent Twigs" were born. We never earned much money, but we did make enough to pay for our equipment. Most of all we had a lot a fun. It was through the activity with the band that I met my first wife.

Wellington is a small town of about 4,500 people. Back then there was a teen night spot on the edge of town called "Danceland." In addition to "Danceland" in Wellington, a few other non alcohol teenage night spots operated in the area. Those places, along with school dances and private parties, provided places for us to play.

In those days rock bands with hit records would promote their records with "barnstorming tours." Bands would travel to four or five of these teenage night spots in one night. They usually arrived in a rented limousine. The band members would only bring their guitars, then they would use the local front band's amplifiers, drums and microphones. These groups would arrive, plug in their guitars and do a set of four songs. The last song would always be the record that was on the charts at that time. They would be at each stop only about twenty-five minutes. Our band fronted for "Tommy James and the Shondels, "Terry Knight and the Pack," (several times) and "The Shadows of Night." It was a great experience and a lot of fun.

One night at "Danceland" when our band wasn't playing, I met a girl. She was attractive and quite a flirt. I was smitten! Tom, our drummer, was with me that night. I told Tom, "I'm going to marry that girl someday."

Tom had seen her around before and he tried to caution me about her. I didn't listen. I forged ahead. Soon I was dating her regularly. I was only a few weeks away from high school graduation. She was just finishing her freshman year at a nearby school. She didn't look like any of the freshman girls I'd seen before!

I was probably fortunate not to have any steady girlfriend during my high school years. The lack of distractions from a serious relationship with a girl, probably aided me in excelling at sports. I dated, but didn't go steady with anyone. The fact that I didn't have my front teeth capped until midway through my senior year probably had something to do with that. Those circumstances made it easy to keep my virginity, not that at that point in my life I necessarily wanted to.

I accepted Christ when I was about twelve years old. I was attending a Pioneers Youth Group in the basement of the First Baptist Church in Wellington. The church had a young pastor who really had a positive influence on me. I did well in the group, winning awards and contests. I even attended a church camp one summer that was located on Kelly's Island in Lake Erie. I received Christ as my savior, but I outgrew the age limits for the Pioneers. Then the young pastor I liked so much moved away. Those two events basically halted my contact with any church.

My mother and father were great people but they were not

Christians at that time. We were the type of family that attended the Methodist Church in Wellington two or three times a year. Usually Easter, and Christmas and sometimes something else would get us to church. I was saved, but I had almost no foundation. My growth as a Christian was stunted. For the next twenty years, I was like the prodigal son. I did my own thing. I created my own theology. I know now, that Christ held on to me, even though I didn't realize it. Like the loving parent He is, He allowed me to make mistakes. I learned that experience is a good teacher, but the tuition is prohibitive.

I was eighteen years old and just out of high school. The girl I loved was fifteen and only going to be a sophomore. She was young, but she didn't look like it. She was fully developed and probably more experienced than I was. That summer we became sexually active.

What a mistake that was! It was like drugs. Once it starts it is hard to control. It was addictive. We were too immature to be involved in such things. Problems in our relationship were glossed over because we both enjoyed the physical contact and the security we had in knowing it was there for us.

There were good times, plenty of them, but there were also signs of trouble. Her insecurities would often manifest themselves. When I left to begin college, I always wanted to return home for two reasons. One was the physical relations we would have. The other reason was because of my own insecurities about our relationship. I realized even then that she needed attention. Her self worth was tied to her appearance. That meant she required frequent affirmation. I knew that if I didn't get back home often to provide it, someone else soon would.

I never really fit into college life at Bowling Green. It was a two hour drive from the university back to Wellington. I would often go back home on the weekends. When I didn't receive my scholarship money for baseball, I wanted to transfer to Baldwin Wallace College, not only because of that, but because I could live at home and commute to college. This allowed me to successfully continue courting my first wife.

Maybe successfully is a bad choice of words. We had quite a few arguments and broke up several times, but the breakups only lasted a month or two and then we would get back together.

I was finishing my junior year of college, getting older and a little more mature. I was beginning to get tired of the constant games she seemed to play. I think she sensed that she was losing her control over me. It was around that time she became pregnant.

This young girl had been the only girl I had ever had sexual relations with. I had rationalized my behavior by believing we were always going to get married. When I finally started to realize we didn't have the great relationship I had deluded myself into believing, it was too late. A baby was on the way.

I was always caving in to her demands, placating her to stay together. When I began to resist, she became adept at making things miserable enough for me until she finally got her way. We had gone together for three bumpy years and I was finally becoming mature enough to begin to realize that we had problems. It was finally beginning to dawn on me that perhaps we weren't a match made in heaven. Now, with a child on the way we would both have to grow up. We would need to work as a team. After all, we did love each other, things would all work out once we were actually married, right?

While attending Bowling Green State University, I had heard about Monroe, Michigan's reputation as being a marriage factory. A place where students would run off and get married. I was twenty-one years old and going to be a senior in college. She was eighteen and just finishing her senior year in high school. We drove to Monroe with some friends and got married. We kept it a secret for over two months. A few weeks after she graduated from high school, we went public with the news.

I'm sure my parents were really hurt and disappointed with me, but they never expressed it, and they remained very supportive. They helped us pay for an apartment in Berea, Ohio where Baldwin Wallace College is located. That allowed us to live on our own while I was able to complete my degree in education. I graduated in the summer of 1970 with a Bachelor of Science degree.

I got a job teaching science at Firelands High School. I was hired as a varsity assistant football coach and supplemented my income further by teaching driver's education. In addition, I passed the state exam and got a real estate license. I sold real estate in the summer.

My wife went to school and became a licensed beautician. She was very good at it and financially we began doing pretty well. We put some sweat equity into fixing up my grandfather's old farm house after he passed away. We rented his old house from the estate and cleaned it and fixed it up to a point where it could be sold. My Dad and aunt and uncles agreed to give us a one acre building lot from the farm, in return for our efforts. That lot became the down payment for building our first new home. It was completed before the end of 1971.

While that was going on in my life, Sherryl graduated from high school in 1970. She went on to a three year nursing school program in Ashland, Ohio. It was at this time that she began to date the man who would become her husband. He was a high school classmate of hers at Wellington. His father was a contractor and he worked with his father after he graduated from high school.

Sherryl was an excellent singer and a beautiful young woman. She entered the Miss Lorain County Pageant at the urging of some friends. It was a prelude to the Miss Ohio Pageant. She finished as the first runner-up. Sherryl tells me that she was told she would have won, except the judges learned that she was engaged. I believe her. She would have received my vote.

The reason she was engaged is a study in applied peer pressure. The two of them had been going steady for some time, but Sherryl was beginning to sense that maybe things weren't exactly right in their relationship. She told me that he proposed to her in front of his large Italian family at their Christmas party. She said she didn't know if she would have accepted his proposal if he had done it privately. It was difficult to say no while she was sitting on his lap with his entire family watching. She accepted and they became engaged.

Since Sherryl didn't have to pursue becoming Miss Ohio, she became a wife in the summer of 1972. In 1973 she graduated from nursing school and became a registered nurse. Now events would start to unfold that would ultimately bring Sherryl and me together for the second time.

# Chapter Three

# *We Meet Again*

❋

*I* finished my first year of teaching and coaching football. The Firelands High School football team tied for their conference championship. With that success, the head coach went on to another coaching position at a larger high school. That school didn't have a teaching position open for me, but the coach helped me get a new teaching and coaching job at another larger high school. It represented about a thirty percent increase in my teaching salary.

My wife and I sold our first new home a year and a half after it was finished. We made enough profit from it to buy a two acre building lot in the country south of Wellington. We had our second new home built there, about four miles southwest of town.

I knew Sherryl's husband from athletic activities we had done together in the past. He was a very good golfer and sometimes we played golf together. We also played basketball on a team that was sponsored by Sherryl's father. At this time, I didn't really know Sherryl at all. My only contact with her had been at the end of her lunch box sixteen years earlier.

Sherryl's husband gave us a good price on building our next new home. We decided to use him as our contractor. During the construction we had to meet with him often. Eventually, our friendly relationship expanded to include Sherryl as well. When our home was finished, we invited them over to see our new home.

This was the second time Sherryl and I met. Since I knew her father, I remembered that she was the little girl that had chased me down and clobbered me with her lunch box years before. This was that first girl that ever showed interest in me. Sherryl sure had changed! She didn't seem like a pest now. She was a self-assured young professional woman. Friendly and engaging, she wasn't nearly as dangerous as she had been when we were younger. We were both married and completely committed to our spouses. We had a nice visit and nothing more. Unfortunately, that wasn't to be the case with our mates.

Shortly after our second home was completed in 1973, I left teaching to take a job selling life insurance. I made the change to placate my wife. She didn't like the hours football coaching required, or the extra curricular activities I had to attend as a teacher. She would never join in or be a part of anything at the school. Her insecurities with these commitments, made succeeding as a teacher and a coach look impossible.

I was recruited by an aggressive district manager into the insurance business. I did fairly well as an insurance salesman, but I quickly began to hate it. Eventually I quit that job to look for something in industrial sales. I wanted a sales position that provided a salary and company car, as well as an incentive program. After a few tough months of searching and interviewing, I finally landed a job I really wanted.

During theses few months of searching for a new career,

I worked as a helper on a Pepsi truck. I tested twice for a position as an air traffic controller, but didn't hear anything back from the government. I was getting a little impatient trying to find something I would really like. So was my wife. We had sold our second new home and made an even bigger profit on it. But we didn't know where we would be living, so we didn't invest in anything else right away.

Things really should have been looking up, when I landed the job with Dearborn Chemical Company. It was a job selling and servicing industrial water treatment. My base salary was considerably higher than anything I had ever received before. I had a company car, expense account, and commissions as well. Even better, I liked my job. It was interesting and challenging. We bought a condominium in Avon Lake, Ohio. It was a better location for the territory I was covering in my new job. Although Avon Lake was only thirty miles from Wellington, the life style there was very different.

My daughter Tracy had been born in December of 1969. Our second child, Kyley, was born in December of 1973. The condominium complex we moved into had a swimming pool, tennis courts and some nice areas for the kids to play. While we were living there, I had my next meeting with Sherryl. My wife invited Sherryl and her husband up to our condo to play tennis. That was really out of character for my wife. Her insecurities bordered on agoraphobia, except when it came to places or situations where she could act flirtatious. I remember she was somewhat flirtatious that day with Sherryl's husband. When our guests left, I was the one who was grilled about what I thought about Sherryl. I really didn't think anything about her. She was married to a friend. She was friendly, sociable and attractive. Anyone could see that, but I didn't have any interest in her. My wife had acted in a flirtatious manner the whole afternoon towards Sherryl's husband. It annoyed me and I could tell it annoyed Sherryl. But after they left, I was being accused of being interested in Sherryl.

It was ridiculous. I hadn't invited them, it was my wife's idea. She acted like a little flirt and now she accused me of being interested in Sherryl. I had to tell my wife that Sherryl wasn't attractive at all, in order just to keep the peace. I was always having to keep the peace.

My wife may have already had some extramarital activity prior to our moving to the condominium complex, I don't know, but it was in that atmosphere that her extramarital activities began for sure. She was attractive and enjoyed all the looks and attention she could gather from other male residents, especially around the swimming pool. She made friends with two or three other women about our age. She told me They were having extramarital affairs. I didn't like what was happening to us. I knew we were in trouble, but I didn't know what to do about it.

Looking back, it is easy to see one of our major problems was that we had no spiritual life together at all. I don't remember us ever going to church. We ignored God completely.

It was about this time, that I had to cover an additional territory for my employer. It meant a little more money and it gave me an excuse for getting us out of the condominium complex. I couldn't sell it, without taking a loss that we didn't need, so we sublet the condo. We moved to a house we rented in Mansfield, Ohio, about two hours southwest of Avon Lake. This put me more in the center of the two territories I had to cover.

One evening just after we moved to Mansfield, while I was driving home, I noticed some lights just south of Rt. 30. I was curious, so I drove over to take a look. It was a baseball game in progress. I parked the car and went over to watch for a few minutes. I was surprised to see the pitcher for one of the teams was a young man from Wellington. He was a left hander that graduated about three years after me. He had been playing in the minor leagues in the Yankee's organization, so I was shocked to see him pitching there that evening. I went over and spoke to him between innings. I learned that he had been released due to an injury, and he was trying to play his way back into professional baseball. He invited me to try out for the team he was on. It was a good caliber of baseball, and the team had several former professional players on it, all trying to play their way back after injuries caused their releases.

I was twenty-seven years old and they called me the old man, but I wanted to try and play again. I went to one practice and they added me to their roster. My wife wasn't very supportive of the idea, but I stood up to her and decided to play anyway. She seldom came to see me play.

It was one of the few times I didn't cave into her. I was glad I didn't. I had a lot of fun. The team won the state championship and finished second in the regional tournament. That qualified us to play in the national tournament in Wichita, Kansas. My boss wouldn't give me the time off to go to the national tournament. I really wish he would have. I hit an even .400 and batted in twenty four runs in the twenty two games I played in. Not bad for an old man who hadn't played in five years.

Our daughter Tracy was almost six years old and our son Kyle was nearing two. We didn't know anyone in Mansfield, and my wife wasn't very happy about having to move. She surprised me one evening by inviting Sherryl and her husband to come down for a visit. They didn't have any children yet. It was a night Sherryl and I still remember thanks to my son Kyley.

Kyle and Tracy had to sleep in the same bedroom. Their bedroom door was just a short distance from the kitchen table we were sitting around that night. I think the four of us were trying to play cards. I had put the kids to bed, but Kyle kept getting out of bed and coming back into the kitchen to join us.

31

Ever notice how much easier it seems to be to make kids mind before you have any kids of you own. I'm sure Sherryl and her husband both thought we were totally inept parents. At first I raised my voice and tried yelling to keep Kyley in bed. That didn't work. Next, I tried spanking him. He still kept getting out of bed and opening the bedroom door. Ultimately, I took one of my neckties and tied the door shut by stretching the tie across to another door and tying them together. It held the door closed, and although Kyle tried to open his door, he finally gave up and went to bed. The episode provided a lot of laughs and a good topic for conversation.

I remember another thing about that evening. We spent a lot of time talking about religion. Sherryl had always been very active in her Assembly of God church. Her husband was now active in the church as well. Eventually he became a board member. His behavior would latter prove that was a position he should not have been entrusted with.

My wife and I said we believed in God, but we didn't think it was necessary to attend church. You know the type we were. I can't imagine how much I grieved the heart of God during those earlier years. I was one of those people that accepted the Bible whenever it agreed with my own opinions. Whenever it didn't, the Bible had to be wrong or mistranslated. Like so many people who think that way, I never realized how obnoxious I was to God. Praise God for his patience and grace.

We talked about tithing. I tried to convince them it was a stupid thing to do. I told them God no longer required it. As if I was someone literate concerning the Bible. Like so many others with an unregenerate mind, I spoke about God and the Bible as if I knew something about them. I didn't. I wouldn't for another five years.

# Chapter Four

# *Major Heartaches*

✳

W e spent a year in the rental home in Mansfield, then we discovered major problems with the people who sublet our condominium. It was 1976 and somehow my marriage had survived seven troubled years. We had problems and things weren't getting any better. We also had two children, and they were the glue that kept me hanging in there, hoping that things would improve. There were already episodes that made me think my wife may have been unfaithful to me, but I was never completely sure. Now we had to move back into the condominium complex and that environment was the last thing we needed.

Many of the young couples living there had one or both partners straying from the ranch, so to speak. The couple we sublet the condo to had divorced without our knowledge. The husband had remained in our property and he let his dog destroy all of our carpeting. We had to get him out of the place and move back in. I was still covering two territories. That made things even worse, because I had to stay overnight at motels about two days a week to do my job.

Looking back, it is easy to see all the negative influences on our marriage. Positive influences were few and far between. The most important positive influence, God, was completely ignored. We had absolutely no spiritual life together at all. The glue our kids provided was real, but it wasn't enough. Maybe it should have been, but it proved not to be. With no higher authority to guide us, we were two selfish mixed-up young people.

There were terrible nights. Nights when my wife went out with one of the other wives in the complex. Nights were she never came home until four in the morning or later. There were even a couple of nights when I had a neighbor watch my kids while I drove around trying to find out where she was and what she was doing. These times are painful to recall. Thankfully, I never do, except now in this attempt to tell our story.

Sherryl was living a similar kind of nightmare in her marriage. She had given birth to a son in June of 1976. Even the responsibility of a child couldn't keep her husband from being unfaithful. Unlike me, Sherryl had God as an active part of her life. Her husband looked like he did too, on the outside, but God wasn't going to keep him from doing whatever he wanted to do. Like me, Sherryl had serious suspicions concerning her mate, but no absolute proof of infidelity.

Positive proof came to me first. I was always being accused of looking for someone else. I even had to avoid looking at someone walking on the sidewalk, because if it was an attractive girl, it would spark minutes of fighting. I loved my children and I loved my wife, but she sure wasn't easy to love. I was about 99% sure she had been unfaithful to me on several occasions. At the same time, I was being accused of infidelity that never existed. For years I had been doing the time, without doing the crime. I was getting sick of it, and it made me look forward to nights when I could stay away from home.

One night while I was away, I called home and through circumstances that I can't even remember, I learned that my kids were staying with a neighbor. I called the neighbor and learned of a phone number my wife left with her in case of an emergency. I called the number and it was a hotel in Columbus, Ohio. My wife was there with one of the husbands from the condo complex.

Finally all doubt was gone. Even so, I didn't want to get divorced. Things didn't get any better. I was hurt and I was discouraged. I was still constantly being accused of doing things that I didn't do, while I knew of my wife's infidelity. Eventually, I did a stupid thing and became unfaithful as well. Maybe I did it just to get back at her. Maybe I did it just to see if I could hurt her as much as she hurt me. Maybe I did it because I was frustrated and lonely from our unhealthily relationship. Whatever reasons I used to justify it, it was **wrong**. My marriage had one foot in the grave and the other on a banana peel. I stopped my infidelity, but things continued to get worse.

Then I made another big mistake. I was at a point where I believed the only chance our marriage had of surviving was for us to start being honest with each other. I thought that if we both confessed our transgressions we could start fresh and rebuild some trust. One evening as our nightly battle began to heat up, I admitted I had strayed. That was not a good idea! My wife never got over the fact that I actually did what she had been accusing me of for years. It was like an unforgivable blow to her vanity. She was supposed to be too beautiful for me to ever desire anyone else. I guess she thought how she treated me, didn't matter. The next four years I continued to try and hold on to our marriage. I didn't want to hurt my children. But our marriage didn't get any better.

We finally found a buyer for our condominium, and I bought a two acre lot five miles south of Wellington. I was always looking for something that would placate my wife. Something that would make my existence easier with her. This third new home was my next effort for something to provide a better life.

Guess who built our new home? Bingo, it was Sherryl's husband. By now it was 1978 and I was to the point where I was trying to save my marriage with things. We finished the nicest home we ever had. Shortly after that, we installed an in-ground swimming pool. We were existing together but I certainly wouldn't have called it living.

Sherryl's marriage was on a similar course. She was living in a nice new home as well, but she was ill. Sherryl had colitis. It was the physical manifestation of her emotional state. She was 99% sure that her husband was cheating on her, but to this point she didn't have the proof. The proof came one snowy winter evening.

Sherryl was going to attend a baby shower at her church. Her husband insisted that she take their small son with her. Sherryl argued that there was no reason why her husband couldn't stay home with his son, or take the child with him if he went anywhere. She left her son, Chad, with his father, and she went to the baby shower.

A short time later, her husband showed up at the church and dropped Chad off. Sherryl smelled a rat. She left her son with a friend and started out into the night to learn the truth. No one knows the agony, the humiliation, or the lack of self esteem a person feels when searching for a straying spouse, unless they have done it themselves. Only those who have lived that nightmare appreciate the depth of despair and heartache it causes.

Sherryl's husband drove a yellow van that was easy to look for. She drove around the village of Wellington and then out by the only motel near the town. Nothing, so she headed for Oberlin, a college town about nine miles to the north. In the parking lot behind the Oberlin Inn she found her husband's van. It was empty. Sherryl parked her car and went into the hotel to see if her husband was registered there. He wasn't, so she did the only thing she could, and went back out to her car and waited. She sat there watching that van, waiting for him to return. When he did, she would be there.

It brings tears to my eyes even now as I write this. Sherryl is too wonderful of a person for anyone to be put her through the pain of a night like that. I know what it is like. Sitting, waiting, watching and crying while your heart breaks. Searching your mind to figure out what you have done to cause this person, the one who had promised to love and honor you, now to callously torture you.

Finally, her husband pulled up driving another person's car. **My car**. My wife was snuggled right up next to him. Sherryl walked up to the car. He saw her coming and rolled the window down. She confronted them and then simply went to her car to go and pick up her son. Her husband cautioned her not to drive crazy and kill herself on the way home. That was nice of him. She had no intention of doing anything like that. When he finally returned home, he confessed to the affair with my wife plus two others.

When my wife got home she confessed to being with Sherryl's husband and going shopping, but nothing more. I knew there was more. The only reason she told me anything was because she thought Sherryl would call me. Sherryl wasn't going to call. She didn't want to do anything that could make my marriage worse, as if anything could. Sherryl had suspected her husband was seeing my wife for some time. After he left their son at the baby shower that night, Sherryl had called my house and asked for my wife. I didn't recognize her voice and didn't really think much about the call. As soon as I said my wife wasn't home, that was all Sherryl needed to prompt her search. She thought her husband was probably meeting my wife. She was right.

It is one thing to suspect your mate of infidelity, it is quite another to positively learn it's true. Not knowing for certain had made Sherryl physically ill with colitis. Now, even though her heart was breaking, she felt a sense of relief to finally know the truth. Sherryl could deal with the truth. She could then and she can to this day. She knew that she wasn't some jealous, insecure, green eyed monster. Her husband had always treated her as if there was something wrong with her for suspecting him. At least now she felt vindicated. There wasn't anything wrong with her. There was something wrong with him.

Sherryl was a Christian so divorce was not her first thought. She had a son and he deserved to have a father. Obviously there were serious problems with her marriage. She wanted to confront them and work them out. She sought help through counseling.

The unfortunate thing about troubled marriages is that usually the most committed partner is the one who wants and accepts counseling. That was the case in my marriage. I wanted help. My wife met any suggestion of professional help with more than just anger. Wrath would be a better choice of words.

Sherryl's husband wasn't as opposed to seeing a counselor as my wife was. He attended one session as only a passive participant. Sherryl learned that her husband's most important needs were to have someone wash his clothes, clean up after him, and cook him meals. He used the Bible to try and support his behavior, indicating that he didn't even see it as wrong. Sherryl wanted companionship, conversation, and affection.

It soon became clear to Sherryl that her husband was not going to change his ways. Monogamy was not on his agenda. Sherryl wasn't going to settle for a life with someone who

wouldn't even honor the sanctity of marriage, theirs or anyone else's.

One cute little boy and six and a half years after their
large beautiful outdoor wedding, Sherryl became someone
she never thought she would be, a divorced woman. This
beautiful, talented, professional woman, who had grown up
in the Christian subculture, had to face the reality of a failed
marriage. She had not discerned her husband's true character. She had been fooled. Experience is a good teacher, but
the tuition is prohibitive.

Sherryl faced her new reality like she faces everything,
head on. She had no bitterness toward her ex-husband. She
just couldn't stay married to him. She remained close to
her former in-laws, and everyone shared in the raising
of their son. They all maintained a good relationship and
tried to minimize the negative impact their mistake had on
their child.

Sherryl had her nursing career and she was not afraid to
be independent. She had held on to her virginity until after
her engagement. This inability to maintain God's standard
had proven costly for her, just as it had for me. She wasn't
pregnant, but the fact that she had relations with her fiancee
made her feel obligated to go forward with the marriage.
She did, even though she was aware of potential problems.

Sherryl and I both learned the hard way. God gave people
instructions about waiting until marriage for their own good.
When people allow sex to enter into their relationships
before marriage, they prevent the relationship from properly
maturing. It can keep faulty couples moving on into marriages that should not happen. This is especially true for
people who are basically very moral, particularly when they
are young.

The human body on the physical plane is essentially a
chemical factory. The hormones that we produce in
response to outside stimuli are a powerful force on our

decision making process, but they are only a force. What makes us different from animals is our will. We have the ability to choose. People often run from God because He reminds them that they are accountable for what they do, and the choices they make. The maturing process in humans occurs when we understand this fact, and accept our responsibility.

Humanity has always had difficulty controlling the gift of sex. I am not a theologian, but I find it significant that God uses the marriage relationship to describe the union between Himself and the Church. We are the Bride of Christ. The intimate relationship that exists in a healthy marriage must be a good picture of how close God wants to be with us. In Genesis, God describes marriage by saying that the man and the woman will become one flesh. Ultimately we must be destined to become so close to God, that He is always part of us.

The year was 1979 and Sherryl had not reached her twenty-seventh birthday yet. She was a single parent with a two year old son. She began her divorced years, and her behavior changed radically. She had tried things one way and it hadn't worked. It not only didn't work, it was a major disappointment. There had to be something better out there. She figured she would eventually find it, she just wasn't sure how to look. The path she took during this time can best be described as "sowing her wild oats."

Sherryl was the oldest of seven children. She had been a model child. An honor student and active church leader, she had been "Miss Goody Two Shoes." She married a man she believed was a Christian. She was terribly disappointed by him. She never lost her faith, but she wandered away from God and the Church. God didn't move, Sherryl did. Her marriage was a bitter disappointment in many ways. The companionship she expected never materialized. Openness and shared feelings were never there. The physical intimacy never came close to fulfilling her expectations. Frustrated would be the appropriate word to describe her.

In her mind, Sherryl had played by the rules, at least most of them, and it hadn't worked. Now she changed the rules. She decided that it was important to learn about the physical side of any relationship before she would ever commit to anyone again. Of course, this is not pleasing to God. Even when we disappoint the Lord, He still holds on to us and protects us. The Lord holds on, even when we let go of Him.

Through long periods of disobedience, God never left Sherryl or me. His love and grace are beyond our comprehension. He had plans for us. Plans we are eternally grateful for.

# Chapter Five

# *Hanging On*

*T*his part of my life is painful to recall. My first marriage lasted almost twelve years by the time my divorce was final. When I finally separated from my wife for good, my children were eleven and seven years old. They had been my only reason for staying married the final five years of my troubled union. I never recall my first marriage except for times like this when I force myself to remember. I can't picture myself coexisting with my first wife for one day now, let alone eleven years. Never the less, those years did happen and they had an impact on many lives.

From 1976 to 1981, good times in my marriage, were few and far between. I think it would be accurate to say I loved my wife, but I didn't like her. She wouldn't let me. She was never content. She would never allow herself to be happy. There was always that next thing she wanted, then maybe life would get better.

My parents had always been very supportive and they had assisted us financially in helping achieve a nice standard of living. Even so, my wife didn't like my parents or any other members of my family. She kept me separated from them as much as possible. Holiday gatherings for my family were always a time of great stress. Either she wouldn't go to them or she would use them as a means to extort something from me in exchange for her attendance.

I was probably just foolish and naïve, but I didn't want to admit how bad things had really become. I would probably be shocked to know the truth about all the things that happened during those years. One episode that occurred around the same time that my wife got involved with Sherryl's husband, had long lasting ramifications.

My wife was a beautician and she was quite good at it. She earned a good income in a job that required her to work only three days a week. In 1977, she developed a slight tremor that caused her head to shake ever so slightly, usually only when she was nervous or tense. It was a problem that no one else seemed to notice, but it was a major problem to her. Her vanity made it much more serious than it was. She saw a doctor about it, and he gave her a prescription for Valium. It was during this time, that she became pregnant. My wife insisted that she couldn't have the baby.

Abortion had been legalized by the infamous Roe vs. Wade Supreme Court decision of 1973. Even though I believe I was saved at age twelve, I was not an active Christian. Never the less, I had serious objections to abortion. I knew it was wrong. My wife insisted that her doctor told her it would be dangerous for her to have the baby while she was using Valium. As I did concerning so many other things, I caved in to placate her concerning this as well. I drove her to an abortion clinic in Akron, Ohio and waited. Physically it was a much rougher day for her than I think she expected. Emotionally, it was a horrible day for me.

We had two children, a girl and a boy. Our marriage was not healthy. My wife just went through an abortion because she said her medication made pregnancy a risk for her. I did not want either or us, or any future child of mine, to ever go through that experience again. Legally, I had no rights to keep her from having the abortion. She knew that, and I knew she would have someone else take her if I refused.

I felt completely helpless. After it happened, I decided the best solution was for me to have a vasectomy. The doctor I went to see about the procedure didn't recommend it. He warned me that I was too young. I was only twenty-eight years old, and he said it was too early in my life to make such a decision. I remember the Doctor saying, "What if you and your wife get divorced. You may want to get married again. A new spouse might want to have children."

That advice proved to be prophetic. Like other times in my life, I didn't listen. I knew that my marriage was not solid, but I was so unhappy in it, that I thought that if we did ever divorce, I would never want to get married again. My immaturity surfaced again. I had the vasectomy anyway.

The Valium was apparently no problem for my ex-wife to have children in the years ahead. She had four more kids after our divorce. The vasectomy proved to be a major problem for Sherryl and me. Experience is a good teacher, but the tuition is prohibitive.

Looking back, the child that was aborted, may not have been mine. The abortion may have been a way to continue hiding her infidelity from me. Perhaps the baby would have made it impossible to hide it any longer. I will never know for sure. One thing I do know, an innocent child lost its life.

After Sherryl caught her husband with my wife, I continued trying to keep my marriage together. It was not easy. I literally developed a headache almost every evening as I made my way home from work. Nothing I did seemed to be able keep arguments from occurring. Nothing we bought seemed to make her happy. I had accepted a new job with a larger water treatment company. It was more money and it required no overnight travel. Things should have been getting better. Instead everything only got worse. In the winter of 1979, my wife filed for divorce and we separated. I moved out of the house and lived in a downstairs bedroom at my parent's home about five miles away.

It was a relief to be away from my wife, but it was torture to be away from my kids. I was not happily married, but I didn't look forward to being divorced. If there was any way the situation could improve, I wanted to stayed married.

We were separated for three months. During that time I was completing the training program with my new employer. The training required four separate one week trips to Philadelphia. The new job and training kept me pretty busy, but they couldn't take away the pain of missing my kids.

The night I flew back from my final week of training, I wasn't in a hurry to return to my parent's house. I wanted to go to my own home, but I couldn't. I was separated. My wife was divorcing me. Instead of going straight to my parent's house, I drove to Elyria and went to a popular pub.

I have never been a big drinker, but I probably did more drinking during those few months, than I have any other period in my life. While I was sitting at the bar, slowly nursing a beer, I saw something I didn't expect. In a booth, sitting with some other girls, there was Sherryl. I just sat there and watched her for a while. I thought about all the things we had both been through. I knew that she had divorced her husband about a year before. To be honest, I was shocked to see her in a pub, drinking a beer. She looked great. She seemed to be having a good time. Her being there was such a surprise to me. She looked happy and very well adjusted.

I knew I was anything but happy and well adjusted. I was deep in self pity over my current situation. No matter how hard I tried, I couldn't keep my eyes from returning to Sherryl. I wondered what would happen if she saw me. I wanted to go over and say hello to her, but I was afraid to.

She was surrounded by friends. She seemed to be there with three other girls, but there were a couple of guys already there conversing with her group. I just stayed put, and watched her from a distance.

Suddenly our eyes met. She saw me. She raised her glass and mouthed hello. I did the same back to her. Then she got up, made her way out of the booth and walked right over to me. That was a pleasant surprise.

"Hi," Sherryl said, and she asked me where my wife was.

"We're separated," I told her. "She's filed for divorce."

"We've got to talk," Sherryl said. She took me by the arm and led me over to an empty booth.

The first time Sherryl and I met she made a lasting impression on me with her lunch box. That had been two decades ago. This time she made a lasting impression on me with her spirit, personality and beauty. The memory of that night remains one of those precious moments that I love to recall.

We had gotten together a couple of other times with our spouses, but we really barely knew each other. We sat in that booth and talked until the place closed. Sherryl filled me in on some of the things that had happened in her life since that night she caught her husband with my wife. I told her about things that had happened to me as well. We were able to put together a few missing pieces in both our histories. Most of all though, she kept asking me about my marriage. She wasn't prying. She was trying to help.

Sherryl lived in a duplex only a mile from my parent's home. She still had a lot she wanted to talk to me about, so she invited me to follow her back to her house. Once there, we continued our conversation in her living room. The impression I came away with that night, was that Sherryl sure could talk. We talked until about 4:00 a.m.. Oh we did kiss and hug a few times, when our stories brought us to tears, but mostly we talked. Sherryl really wanted to know where my thoughts were concerning my wife. Did I still love my spouse? Did I want to save the marriage? By the time I left that night, Sherryl had determined that I did want to stay married. She understood that I didn't want my kids to be hurt by divorce. She encouraged me to do everything I could to save my marriage. Sherryl knew that divorce was never the best answer and not what God wanted. She also knew, that sometimes it couldn't be avoided. In addition to learning that Sherryl really liked to talk, I learned something else about her that night, she was a very nice person.

The following morning was a Saturday, and as fate would have it, I got a phone call from my wife. She wanted to stop the divorce proceedings. She asked me to come back home. When I got off the downstairs phone and headed up the steps to my parent's living room, I remember my father leaning over the railing. He asked me who called. I told him it was my wife and she wanted to call off the divorce. Dad asked me what I was going to do. I told him I was going back home.

My dad never barged into my life. He was never one of those fathers who tried to talk to my coaches or intercede on my behalf. He was always supportive. When he offered advice, it was always only offered, never imposed. He offered his advice on where I should attend college, and I wished I would have followed it. He offered his concerns about my relationship with my wife, before we had married. His concerns proved to be valid. Now he offered me these words, "Gordy, I don't think it is ever going to work out, but it's your family and you have to do what you think is best."

My wife and I had been separated for three months. It was the first time lawyers had actually been contacted by either of us. I was hoping my wife finally wanted to make our relationship better. Maybe she realized what we would lose if we stayed on the destructive course we were on. I hoped that our relationship would change course. During the year to come, those hopes were dashed.

Within three months of my return home, my wife started

to run around with a new circle of friends. I don't even know how she originally linked up with them, but she did. She befriended a woman that was divorced who was several years older than her. Ultimately she began to see this woman's brother or brother- in-law (I'm not sure which). A man at least ten years older than I was. We had a confrontation about what she was doing. I thought I made it clear that it had to end.

On my thirty-second birthday, May 24th 1980, I had planned to take my wife and children out for the evening. My wife insisted on going to a graduation party for the nephew of this woman that was her new friend. She said she would take our ten year old daughter with her and just stay for a few minutes and drop off a card. I wasn't happy about it, but she said they were friends and I shouldn't be worried. She would just stop in and leave the card and then head right back home.

I waited at home with my six year old son for her return. Time crept by and she didn't come home. My anger started to burn. It was my birthday. We were supposed to be going out with the kids, together, as a family. She didn't come home. She had left before 6 p.m. and now it was getting dark and after 8:30 p.m.. The plans for the evening were shot. I wasn't going to wait any longer. I got my son into the car and off we went to the lady's house.

Surprise, the graduation party wasn't at her house, but at the house next door. It belonged to the man my wife had been seeing. The woman's nephew that was graduating, turned out to be his son.

The man's house sat back about a hundred yards from the main highway that runs north and south into Wellington. The driveway was filled with cars and the overflow parking was out front on the side of the main road. I parked just off the highway and told my son to wait in the car. Kyley could see how angry I was, and I was sure he knew not to disobey me and try to leave the vehicle. I locked the doors and headed up the driveway towards the party that was going on outside, in front of the man's garage.

My anger level was probably at an all time high that night. As I got closer to the party, I found my wife arm in arm with the guy she wasn't supposed to see anymore. I walked up, took hold of her arm and told her to get our daughter Tracy, and come home.

Suddenly, the man she was with, starts bouncing around in front of me with his fists up, making like Mohammed Ali. To tell you the truth, I wasn't even mad at him! I definitely didn't like him, but as far as I was concerned, he wasn't the problem. Just then, out pops his fist and he hit me flush on my face. I was so angry, and so pumped up with adrenaline, that I didn't feel a thing. I didn't want to fight this guy, but now I didn't have a choice. I remember kind of shrugging my shoulders as if to convey the thought of "why did you have to go and do that." Then I shot out my left arm and hit him. I was shocked when he fell right to the ground.

Now, I am not a fighter. I was an athlete, and I loved to play sports aggressively, but I didn't get into fights. I never saw the point. Most of the kids I saw get into fights ended up shaking hands later, and walking off as friends. It didn't make much sense to me. I figured the only time to ever get into a fight, was when you had no alternative, when you weren't going to shake hands and be friends afterwards. I hadn't been in a fight since the second grade. Believe me when I tell you, it was a very pleasant surprise when that one left hand ended the whole thing. I started to walk back to my car when I was jumped from behind. Not by one man, but by the party. I was knocked down to my hands and knees. People were on top of me, beside me, all around me. I could feel them holding my arms and feet down. I could tell someone was punching me in the back of my head. I couldn't move, and I was being pummeled, but it didn't hurt! Finally,

I heard a voice say, "Get off him. That's his wife."

The pile moved and I was released. I stood up and looked at my wife. I found my daughter and walked to my car with her. When I got to the car, my son was crying in the back seat. He had seen enough family arguments to know that this time something was really wrong. I opened the door and put Tracy in the car. Then I reassured them that everything was going to be all right. I closed the back door on the passenger side of the car and walked around the front to get in. It wasn't going to be that easy.

There to meet me was a circle of senior boys, among them the son of the man I had just decked. This was the boy the party was for. He began bouncing around with his fists up, just like his father had done. I told him this didn't have anything to do with him. He hit me flush on the face. I still didn't feel a thing. I shot out my left arm again. It made contact! Down he went, flat on the highway. It scared me. I didn't want to hurt this boy. I told his friends, "Just pick him up and get out of my way. This is none of your business!" Fortunately for everyone, they did what I asked.

I learned something about myself that night, and about how my body works. I have always known I had a temper. I avoided fights because they just never made sense to me. Usually fights are between two people that really don't want to hurt each other. I felt that if you were concerned about the condition your opponent would be in after the fight, then you shouldn't fight at all.

That night I had been forced to fight. I was angry and filled with adrenaline. I was not angry at the people I fought. I was angry with my wife. I was so angry that when they hit me, I felt no pain. I was surprised when my return blows had flattened both father and son. My wife had brought my emotional state to a place where I realized I could be dangerous. Driving home, I decided it was an emotional state I would never let her take me to again. It dawned on me that our marital problems had become so bad that now they could hurt other people. The boy graduating hadn't done anything, but he could have been seriously injured. I was sick of it. The games were over. I wasn't going to play anymore.

I drove home, my kids crying, sensing that things were very wrong. I was ashamed of what they had just seen. This had to stop.

My wife got home just after I did. She probably was expecting our usual loud argument. I had done my fighting already. I wasn't going to fight anymore. When she came in I asked her to sit down and talk with me. I told her that I was never going through anything like that again. If she wanted a divorce it was fine with me. If she wanted to be married, there would be no more fooling around. I said if she started playing those games again, I would leave. There would be no more yelling or fighting. It would simply be over, completely over. It only took until early December of 1980, for it to begin again. When it did, I never raised my voice. I just told her to get a lawyer, and I moved out.

It was time to face reality. My wife would never be happy married to me. I had to get away from her before someone got seriously hurt or killed. It meant my relationship with my children would never be the same. I knew she wasn't the wife I had hoped for, but I thought she was a good mother. I really thought she would always keep my children's best interest at heart. I assumed the best. That was a mistake.

# Chapter Six

# God Helps
# in Spite of Us

*I* told you this book was about miracles. Up until now you've read about some interesting circumstances in Sherryl's and my life, but they hardly qualify as miraculous. Definite miracles were to come, but what happened right after I knew my marriage was over, seemed like a miracle to me. It came in the form of the best friend I ever had. Finding a great friend when your life is in crisis is wonderful enough. When the friend comes in the form of a 5'6" beautiful blonde, to me that qualifies as a miracle.

One of Sherryl and my favorite movies is "When Harry Met Sally." We like it because it reminds us of our relationship. Just as the characters played by Meg Ryan and Billy Crystal became best friends before they got married in the movie, so did Sherryl and I. Everyone should marry their best friend (and they should be the opposite sex).

It had been a year since the night I talked to Sherryl. I

wanted to see her again. I hoped she hadn't gotten engaged or married. The day after I moved out of my home and back into my parents' house I called her. Thank God she was home. I told her I was separated again and would like to talk to her. I thought that would work because I sure remembered how much she liked to talk. It did work. I went over to see her that evening at her place.

In my ranking of pleasant memories, that night is right near the top. Sherryl and I did talk and talk and talk. Her objective was to find out where I really was. She wanted to know what had happened and what had changed since the year before. I told her. After a while she knew that my marriage was over. She knew that I was never going back. We both knew there was nothing to go back to.

I can't explain it. Right from the start, Sherryl and I could honestly talk about anything. It had been that way the year before, and this time was just the same. I had the most open conversation I ever had with anyone. I always had to guard everything I said in my marriage, because anything could lead to a fight. The open conversation we shared that night made me feel like I had just been liberated from under a rock. We were friends.

I had accepted Christ as a youngster but I hadn't grown spiritually. God and I had met long ago, but we had been separated ever since. God had tried to speak to me for years through the conscience He provides us all. I learned to ignore that conscience when I didn't like what it was telling me. I created my own morality. A morality created with rationalization, selfishness and ignorance. Unfortunately, I was like most people. I was on the throne. I saw God as my cosmic servant. I only spoke with Him when I needed something.

Sherryl's journey was almost the opposite of mine. She also had accepted Christ as a youth, but she had grown up in the church. In fact she grew up in several churches. Her mother was Catholic, her father became a Pentecostal and she also spent a lot of time in Baptist youth groups. Sherryl grew up in the Christian subculture. She had followed most of the rules and suffered bitter disappointment anyway. She never became angry at God over her divorce. She simply stepped away from Him. Her first husband had fooled her. He hadn't been a Christian when they started dating, but he behaved as though he became one. Before they married she believed he was a Christian. To win her hand, he became active in her church. After their marriage his actions certainly didn't line up with the Christianity she knew. Her Church family had disappointed her as well. God was still there, but Sherryl distanced herself from Him. She never stopped believing. She simply stopped complying with His advice. She would experience the world's way for a while.

Neither Sherryl nor I knew it at the time, but we had a hidden ally quietly working on our behalf. It was my sister Glenda. Glenda was eight years older than me. She was the first in my family to mature in a real relationship with Christ. It was her prayers and persistency that finally brought my mother and father to a saving knowledge of the Lord. It was her prayers and witnessing that finally began to reach my unregenerate mind. We hadn't been close because my marriage had kept me further from my family than I wanted. Even so she had kept me in her prayers. Glenda knew Sherryl as well. She had often thought we should get together if my marriage ever failed. Quietly in the background she had been a secret advocate on behalf of both of us. Thank God.

Sherryl's friendship was a lifeline for me. I was so disillusioned about marriage. When I finally gave up on mine, I figured I would never want to be married again. Legally my divorce was not too difficult. It was not contested by either of us. The divorce was completed in three months. I just wanted it to be over. My wife made one attempt to stop the process shortly before it became final. I really don't know why, because nothing had changed. The fact that I had such a good friend in Sherryl helped me realize that a much healthier relationship was possible with a woman. The divorce became final in early March of 1981.

The legal phase of the divorce was complete. The pain the divorce would cause was far from over. I hoped for the best from my former wife regarding our children. I thought she had always been a decent mother. I felt secure in the fact that she loved the children as much as I did. I thought that would mean we would both keep their best interests at heart. I was wrong. It was a mistake that I was never able to correct.

My former wife's problems were more serious than I ever realized. My first indication of trouble began with problems concerning my visitation rights. I had always been very close to my children. I was the parent that went to parent teacher conferences, drove them to their activities and spent time playing with them. Now, suddenly my children started to balk at coming with me for my visitation.

I knew the reason. My ex-wife was holding them emotionally hostage. I shouldn't have been surprised. She had done it to me for eleven years. I suppose I thought she cared enough about the kids that she wouldn't do anything that would hurt them. I was wrong. The kids became her one remaining tool to hurt, manipulate and frustrate me. Their welfare was secondary to her need to punish me and continue controlling me.

I had a difficult time realizing the severity of my former wife's problems until a terrible day in mid May of 1981. In early December of 1980 I went to my son Kyle's parent teacher conference. His first grade teacher was Mrs. King. She was a very nice young lady. I knew Kyley really liked her as his teacher. I will never forget what she told me that day, because as a parent it was just too good to be true. Mrs. King said that Kyle was doing very well. She said he was tops in the class academically. It was what she said next that was so amazing.

"I shouldn't tell you this," Mrs. King said, "but your son is such a joy. All the teachers love him. If I had twenty more kids just like him, I would do this job for nothing." It was not your typical parent teacher conference, but it wasn't a total surprise. I knew Kyle was getting good grades. I also knew he had a very cute personality. It was just very nice to hear that his teachers felt the same way.

It was only about a week after that conference that I learned my wife was involved in extramarital activities again. That was when we separated for the final time. I moved back to my parents' house. My parents' home was only about six miles from my house. It shouldn't have been difficult to see my kids, but it was.

I know that as a Christian I am commanded to forgive. I honestly still find it hard not to resent my ex-wife for how she used and manipulated my children. They, like all kids, suffered greatly when we divorced. They were made to suffer far more than necessary. The emotional manipulation their mother put them through was easy to see and heartbreaking to watch. If they acted like they wanted to go with me for visitation, their mother would torment them. If they indicated that they had a good time with me, she would make their lives miserable. This wasn't done physically, but emotionally. There were many times the kids simply wouldn't go with me when they were supposed to. The times they would come, they would always act like they didn't want to, until we got out of sight of their mom. Once they knew they were far enough away from her, so that she couldn't possibly see them, they were fine. We would have nice times together, right up until about an hour before I would need to take them back. Then they would start to distance themselves. They would begin to prepare to placate their mom by telling her whatever she wanted to hear. This pattern never changed.

The depth of the problem became painfully clear a terrible day in mid May of 1981. It was a Friday. I drove over to get the kids for their weekend visitation just after they got home from school. My ex-wife came out to the car when I drove into the driveway. She was smiling. "You're going to have to talk to your son." She said. "He doesn't want to go with you. Oh, by the way, he flunked the first grade."

I was in shock. How could he flunk the first grade? Worse yet, why was his mother acting happy about it? I drove straight to his school hoping that Mrs. King would still be there to talk to. She was. What she told me made me realize that I had made a terrible mistake not fighting for custody when we divorced.

"Kyley changed drastically right after you left home." Mrs. King said. "He use to always talk about his dad. He hasn't talked about you at all since you left home. His work started to fall off, but the major reason he failed is because he missed so much school." His mom hadn't even been sending him to school!

When I left the school I was livid. I knew My ex-wife had problems, but I never believed she would intentionally harm her own kids. I never believed she would be laughing about her son flunking school. I never believed she would not send her children to school. When I got back to what had been my house, we had a loud argument in the driveway. I made Tracy and Kyley come with me and left for the weekend. That Sunday evening when I brought the children back, the guy my former wife had living with her, came out and got into my car. He was much younger than my ex-wife and quite a bit bigger than me. He scolded me for yelling at her. Then hit me once, with a cupped hand, right over my left ear. It caused a piercing pain that I had never felt before. I didn't fight with him. I probably would have lost, but when he said that he had killed more people than I had, fighting seemed like a really bad idea. When he got out of my car I went straight up to the

Wellington police station and filed a complaint.

The nightmare that I was living was going to get worse, much worse. The blow to my head had punctured my left eardrum. That was not so bad, but my complaint had led me to discover who this man was. My wife had thrown our marriage away for a twice convicted felon. That was bad enough, but the county sheriff's department informed me that they considered him to be a very dangerous fellow. He was someone they felt was involved in many more illegal activities than just the two he had been convicted of.

By this time Sherryl had become the best friend I ever had. Even though we had a great relationship and were very close, I don't think she could fully understand how much I began grieving over the situation I had allowed my children to be in.

I went straight to my attorney. My one consolation was that I believed the situation would allow me to get custody of my kids. I was mistaken. I tried to get custody and got nowhere. I had the misguided idea that the domestic court system had the best interest of children at heart. I would come to believe just the opposite. Everything that I experienced indicated to me that they wanted children in trouble. It must represent job security for them. If not, how do you explain why I couldn't get custody from my ex-wife. She was on Aid to Dependent Children. She was living with a man who was a convicted felon. She hadn't bothered to send my son to school. She was not obeying court ordered visitation. None of that mattered to the court.

In subsequent attempts to regain custody after Sherryl and I were married, we were always denied. Later we bought my home back from my ex-wife. She needed the money for legal fees. She was trying to prevent her new husband from a third conviction. We were still denied custody. When her new husband was convicted and returned to prison, the court said he was not a bad influence, because he was out of the house. When he was out of prison they still denied us. My kids failing in school didn't matter either. Nothing seemed to matter. The court just left them with her.

It has also been difficult for me to forgive the court system. As a result of the court's indifference, both of my children never graduated from high school. The domestic court never did anything that benefited my kids. As far as the legal system was concerned, unless my children were physically or sexually abused, nothing warranted my wife losing custody. It never mattered that they did terribly in school, were on welfare, or that the step-father was a felon.

Once my children and ex-wife were in a van when the police captured her husband after he had escaped from prison. She had helped him escape. I was never notified about the incident by the police or the court. I only learned that my children had been in the van after pursuing information a friend provided. The court never prosecuted her for helping him escape from prison. The court never regarded her unfit even after that. I never regained custody. I wish someone could explain why.

Maybe you can see why it has not been easy to forgive my ex-wife. It doesn't matter how difficult it is. We must forgive. I must forgive her and the court. I have also had to overcome resentment towards my children. If they had the backbone to just say that they wanted to come and live with me, I probably could have gotten them back. They never did. I understand why. They knew that if they did, their mother probably would have completely disowned them. They didn't want to risk that and I understand. They knew they didn't have to fear that from me. I realize that and I forgive them, but they paid a price to placate their mother. It was a shame.

# Chapter Seven

# *Helped and Harmed*

In many ways my life from the time I moved out of my home in December of 1980, until the discovery of how bad the situation was that my children were in, was a dichotomy. I had found a wonderful friend in Sherryl. She taught me that the type of relationship I had always wanted with a woman was really possible. On the other hand I was terribly guilt ridden and frustrated concerning my children and what was happening to them.

Sherryl was exactly the opposite of my ex-wife. Both were attractive women but my former wife was insecure and antisocial. Especially when it came to my family. Sherryl was self assured. She joined into activities with my family right from the start. I enjoyed her family as well.

Sherryl quickly became the recreational partner I had always hoped for. She taught me how to snow ski. We both enjoyed bowling. We both played softball and she loved to play cards with my family. We bowled in a couples league with my mom and dad, Glenda and her husband and my niece and nephew.

I felt free to be myself for the first time since 1966 when I began dating my ex-wife. I joined a men's bowling league with my dad and brother in law. I coached a hot stove baseball team. I played fast pitch softball with Sherryl's brother. I was really enjoying my life for the first time in years.

Sherryl bowled on a women's team with my mother, her former mother in law, her mother, and her sisters. She pitched for a slow pitch woman's team. My folks started going to all her games. Eventually, our friendship even survived my coaching her softball team.

A skiing trip Sherryl took me on is one of the fondest memories of my life. We went to Holiday Valley in New York between Christmas and New Years in 1980. I had only separated from my wife a couple of weeks earlier. Sherryl had already become a good friend. We talked about skiing and I told her that I had never done it, but always wanted to try. She said she would take me.

Holiday Valley was about a six hour drive from home. The long ride only gave us more time to do what Sherryl seemed to like to do the most, talk. It was great and we got to know more and more about each other. I doubt that Sherryl knew it at the time, but she did something on that ski trip that really impressed me. She made a point of the fact that she would help me for a while and then she was going to go off and enjoy herself skiing other slopes while I got the hang of it. It showed me how secure she was.

That is exactly what Sherryl did, too. When we got on the slopes, she stayed with me through my equipment struggles and helped me while I inched my way over to the beginner's slope. The lift on this slope was a T-bar type. It was basically just a rope lift with a T-bar that allows two people to place the bar behind their legs. The bar then pushes the skiers up the slope while they ride on their skies. Now, Sherryl was a decent skier but not an expert. She had only been skiing a handful of times herself, but she was way ahead of me in her ability at this point.

I probably won't be able to tell this story so that I paint the picture well enough, but I want you to get to know what Sherryl is like. We finally got into position as our turn to catch the T-bar came. It wasn't pretty, but we started up the slope. I was totally satisfied with how we were proceeding, but I could see Sherryl was giving me the once over. While I was just content to be moving up the hill, Sherryl needed to point out that I was sitting too much on the bar. She said I needed to move the bar down more to the top of the back of my legs. I tried to convince her that I would improve on the next trip. She insisted that I make the adjustment right then. We were about half way up the hill when I tried to comply with Sher's wishes. I lost my balance and started to fall. I desperately held on trying to avoid the failure that now was imminent. By holding on, I pulled the entire lift rope over to the right and down to within inches of the ground. Sherryl and I not only fell, but I had succeeded in knocking everyone off the lift above and below us. As we made our way back to the bottom, I experience my first encounter with lift rage. Several people were not happy with me.

I withstood the embarrassment and we tried again. This time Sherryl accepted my position on the bar. Since she had skied before, she had the proper kind of clothing. She wore an orange pair of ski bibs and had a ski jacket. I had on jeans and a corduroy jacket. My clothes were not water resistant like hers. She warned me that could be a problem. I had always been good at athletics so I didn't expect to fall much. That proved to be overly optimistic on my part.

When we reached the top of the beginner's hill and slid away from the lift, Sherryl lost her balance making her first little turn and fell to the ground. I don't know how she did it, but she got herself all tangled up. I was up on my skies watching her and my laughter started and just continued to build and build. She couldn't get up. To this day I have no idea how she did it, but she was in a knot. I remembering watching her trying to untangle herself and thinking how she looked like Olive Oil in a Popeye Cartoon. I laughed until it hurt. We eventually had to take off her skies and poles in order to get her untangled.

Sherryl really was a good skier. She probably didn't fall down three more times the entire day. I, on the other hand, quickly graduated to the intermediate slopes. I fell often, usually by design, in order to keep from going totally out of control. She skied with me some of the time, but true to her word, she went off and skied more difficult slopes than I wanted any part of. It was a shame she didn't just stay where she could watch me. She would have had a lot of laughs.

I am telling you about this skiing trip to help you under-stand the difference between Sherryl and what my first wife was like. To begin with, my first wife probably would never have gone skiing. If I ever could have convinced her to go, I would have had to buy her all new clothes and the perfect skiing outfit. My first wife would have been more concerned with her appearance than with any physical activity. If she would have taken a lesson, she would have flirted with the instructor. My first wife would have never allowed me to go off and ski without her, and she would have quickly retreated to the lodge and worried about looking pretty. The actual skiing would have been totally unimportant to her.

Sherryl was just the opposite. She was there to ski. She didn't worry about her looks, she knew she looked good. She didn't want me to inhibit her or her inhibit me from hav-ing a good time. What a wonderful change this relationship was for me.

I must have had more than one guardian angel watching over me that day. Only divine intervention could have kept me from permanent damage. I knew my own limitations. I was trying not to do more than I was capable of. Never the less, it seemed as though I managed to have several brushes with death anyway. Most of my falls were controlled falls to keep me from going too fast or risking a collision with an innocent skier. Even so, I had adventures were I couldn't make turns and had near misses with trees. My most spectacular crash came when I was trying to be very conservative. There was a large intermediate slope that at the top was steeper and icier than I wanted to tackle. I decided I would play it safe and take a novice slope from the top that curved around and came back into the intermediate slope further down the hill where it wasn't nearly as steep. The plan was flawless. The execution wasn't.

Where the novice slope curved around it got steeper and was icy. I didn't make the turn. Suddenly I found myself heading straight down a very steep expert slope! What made matters even worse was that some idiot had planted slalom poles all over the place. I was completely out of control, going somewhere near the speed of sound. I was collecting slalom poles under both arm pits as my life flashed before me. When I broke the sound barrier I knew things weren't going to get any better. I figured falling then was better than waiting until later. It was a spectacular fall. I tumbled down the hill about three hundred yards with slalom poles flying out from under my arms every fifty yards or so. I know it was quite a fall because when I eventually came to a stop, skiers from all over the place came rushing over to administer last rights. I guess maybe this was a miracle too, now that I think about it, because I wasn't hurt. With the exception of having snow in every crevice of my body, I was fine.

I wish Sherryl had seen that fall. She would have had to have been impressed by my indestructibility.

Sherryl and I ended the day skiing the longest intermediate slope together that evening. With her proper clothing she was warm and fine. I ,on the other hand, literally had my wet gloves freeze to the safety bar on the ski lift. My clothes were soaked from the snow I had removed from several slopes. With icicles hanging from my mustache, we headed down the mile long gentle slope one last time. I had one goal in mind. I was going to make it all the way down without falling. I wanted to impress this young woman with how much I had progressed in one day.

We started down. I was doing quite well. I had to stop to rest a couple of times. I was demonstrating to Sherryl how I had learned to keep under control without having to fall down. I could turn. I could stop. I could slow down or speed up as I desired. I was wet, cold and embarrassingly improperly dressed, but I was going to show this woman that I was an athlete.

We had progressed to a point where the bottom of the hill was only about two hundred yards away, but my legs were too tired. I turned and came to a stop to rest. Sherryl had gone on ahead and was at the bottom of the hill looking back up at me. It looked like I just laid down on the snow on purpose. It was the least of all the falls I had taken the entire day but it hurt my knee. Not too severely and not permanently, but at that moment it hurt enough that I couldn't get up for quite awhile. Sherryl didn't even realize I was hurt. She went on into the lodge and returned her rented skies. Eventually I was able to get up. I did manage to get back to the lodge without having the ski patrol haul me in, but it took a while. Sherryl wondered what kept me. When I told her I had hurt my knee she felt bad that she had left me. I was sore, wet and freezing. My knee hurt. Even so, it had been one of the best days of my life.

I was having many happy days during this period of time. Sherryl encouraged me to date other woman. She was concerned that I was just getting attached to her because I was on the rebound. While we saw a lot of each other, we both still dated others. Sherryl was not in a hurry to get married again. She was afraid. She had been burned once and she wasn't going to get burned again. We were good friends but she wasn't going to let it be more than that. While the morality we each had shaped for ourselves allowed us to have physical relations, neither of us were allowing that to make us commit emotionally.

For me, the time from December of 1980, when I separated from my wife through May of 1981, was a period of tremendous contrasts. I was enjoying my own life while I was heartbroken over my children's lives. Sherryl, my family, and my new job made me very happy. The constant battle to see my kids, and the situation I knew they were in, tormented me. The fact that I could be happy without them seemed to make it even worse.

While I was completely free from ever wanting to be reunited with my ex-wife, I was not completely free from her ability to yank my chain. She knew that nothing she said or did mattered to me anymore. She used the only thing left to try to control me, our children. Her total callousness towards me and her willingness to harm her own children just to hurt me, took its toll. Her ability to control my kids to a point where they were unwilling to see me just so they could keep the peace with their mom, seemed to eat at me as well. At the same time things were good, they were terribly bad. I was more of a mess than I, or anyone else knew. My ex-wife was wearing me down. Every time I tried to stay part of my kids' lives she shot me with another emotional bullet. I was in trouble. Deep trouble and I didn't even know it.

# Chapter Eight

# *God Talked, I Listened*

*It was early June of 1981. My kids' school year had just ended. It was only a few days before that I had learned of my son failing first grade. My encounter with my ex-wife's live in lover had made me aware of his criminal back ground. I had already learned that I still couldn't get custody of my children. I felt helpless. I wanted them with me.

I had made plans for my kids to spend the first week of summer with me. It was about dusk on a beautiful Sunday evening when I drove over to pick up Kyley and Tracy. When I turned into the driveway, instead of my children coming out packed and ready to go, my ex-wife walked out to the car. "The kids don't want to go with you," she said. "I told them they had to, but they said they won't go. I don't know what's wrong with them. I don't know why they hate to be with their father. I'd like to get rid of them for a few days, but they just won't go."

It was easy to see that my former wife was enjoying herself. As much as I didn't want to let her know how each word was hurting me, she could sense the pain she was causing. She had stuck the knife in, now she was going to twist it off. "Tracy says she not going. When I tell her she has to, she cries and runs away from me. I can't make her go," my ex-wife said.

Tracy was eleven and I knew she could be easily manipulated by her mom. Kyle was seven. I thought he would stand by me, even with all the pressure I knew his mother would put him under. I thought he would come with me if I could just get him into the car to talk with me alone, away from his mom. I told his mother to have Kyley come out and talk to me. I stood my ground and waited until my ex-wife finally went in the house and sent Kyle out to the car. He reluctantly came out and got in the front seat next to me. "I don't want to go with you dad," he said. Then with a cold hard voice he said, "I don't love you anymore, I love (and he inserted the name of the man my wife had replaced me with) now.

The pain I experienced at that moment far exceeded anything I had ever felt before in my life. I was heartbroken. I also was angry and disappointed in my children. I knew this wasn't the way they really felt. I understood why they were treating me like this. Even so, I hoped they wouldn't totally cave in to the controlling pressures from their mother. They were placating her now, doing exactly what I had done for years. It was their effort just to get along with their mom. I think they figured that I understood. They probably thought I was strong enough to handle the pain. I wasn't.

I told Kyley he could get out of the car. I backed out of the driveway. By the time I reached the road, I was crying uncontrollably. With tears rolling down my face I started down the road and headed for my parents' home. I was tired. I was so unbelievably tired. An exhaustion settled over me like a heavy wet blanket. I don't know if I said it out load or

I just thought it, but I remember thinking "I can't take this anymore. I'm just too tired."

Most people who know me probably think I am the type of person that would never contemplate suicide. Normally they would be right, but at that moment in my life, I was dangerously suicidal. I say that because I didn't want to end my life to hurt anyone. I was just so tired of it all. The exhaustion was smothering me. I needed rest. I wanted peace. A couple of miles ahead, across from the entrance to Findley State Park, was a house with a huge tree in the front yard. The tree was just off the road. It was easy to reach. I started to speed up. When I came to the tree I would drive into it. This time I did say it out loud, "God, I just can't take it anymore. I give up."

Even now, twenty years after that moment, my eyes tear up when I think about what happened next. I know I will never be able to describe it accurately enough to convey the life changing impact the next few moments had on me. Right at the instant that I totally gave up, at the only time in my life that I completely surrendered control, a voice spoke to me.

"I STILL LOVE YOU," the voice said.

"What?" I said aloud as I turned and looked for someone in the back seat of the car.

"I STILL LOVE YOU. THIS IS AS BAD AS IT IS GOING TO GET FOR YOU. SOMETHING WILL HAP-PEN TOMORROW TO PROVE THAT EVERYTHING I SAY TONIGHT IS TRUE," the voice said.

That was the total direct conversation. It lasted only a few seconds, but an unbelievable amount of information was transferred to me in those moments. I can't adequately describe the voice to you. I heard it, but I'm not sure I heard it through my ears. It was not a thought. It definitely hadn't originated from me. It defied description. But as wonderful as the voice had been, it was what I knew instantly about the person speaking to me that has changed me forever.

I was overwhelmed by the love that flooded over me. I had been crying uncontrollably. As soon as I heard the voice, I was instantly aware that the person speaking to me was hurting more for me than I was. The empathy washed over me like a tidal wave. Immediately I stopped crying. My crying stopped because I felt so bad over all the pain I was causing the person speaking to me.

As He spoke, we had this secondary communication. It was like a meeting of our thoughts. As I listened to what the voice was saying, I was thinking "Who are you? Who are you?" The answer to my thought question came right back to me, almost like it was engraved on my mind. "Read the Bible, that's who I AM." He answered me in the same way I asked the question, in thought, not audibly like the rest of the conversation.

I drove right past the tree. Any thought of turning into it had vanished. I drove another mile ahead to a place where I could pull off the road and replay what had just happened to me.

Jesus had just spoken to me. I knew it wasn't an angel. It wasn't my own thoughts. It wasn't any demon trying to trick me. It was Jesus Himself. How did I know that? Because of the love. The love that enveloped me goes beyond description. It surpassed life itself. It could only be from someone who loved me enough to die for me. For the first time in my life, I understood how much I meant to God. I was humbled beyond words. I was not tired anymore. Exhaustion had been replaced by exaltation and exhilaration. "He is really there and He knows me! He knows everything! He is going to do something!" I told myself. I sat for a while in the car and just bathed in the experience. Then I had to go and tell somebody. I wanted to tell Sherryl. I drove over to her house. She was home. I started to explain to her what had just happened. I was disappointed because the magnitude of the event seemed lost on her. It wasn't Sherryl's fault. I just couldn't adequately relay the experience. Sherryl was more concerned over my intention to drive into the tree. She was upset that I would even think of such a thing. That concern overshadowed my effort to try to make her understand who spoke to me.

I went home. I wanted to remember every detail of the conversation, the voice, and the thoughts we exchanged. I didn't want anything else clouding my memory or interfering with my thoughts. When I got to my parents' house, they were expecting the kids to be with me. "Where are the kids?" Mom asked.

"They wouldn't come," I told her.

Mom could see I had been crying. "Are you all right?" She asked.

"I'm OK Mom, everything is going to be all right. I'll tell you about it in the morning. I just want to go to bed now." I went to my room and just replayed everything over and over in my mind. I couldn't fall asleep. I read the Bible and just kept reviewing what had just happened. It was the wee small hours of the morning before sleep finally came.

For the first time in my life I realized that God is a person. He is a being very much like us. He loves us with a love that dwarfs anything we realize. He wants to be with us, to be intimate with us, but He never barges in. He must be invited. The more we can get out of ourselves and give up trying to control everything ourselves, the closer He can be with us. I have had other spiritual experiences in the years following this event, but I have never actually heard God again like I did that night. I think I know why. It is because that night was the only time in my life that I totally gave up control. At the instant I let go, He took hold. Now I knew that God was real. I still had a lot to learn. I wanted to know more about the One who spoke to me.

The next morning I woke up to the sound of the telephone

ringing. There was a phone just outside my bedroom door in the downstairs hallway. My dad answered it upstairs. "Gordy it's for you. It's your boss." Dad said. Those words sent a twinge of apprehension through me. With all the recent problems I was having with my ex-wife and visitation, I had not been very productive at work. I was afraid he was calling to let me go. Ray, my boss said "Gordy, what have you got planned for today?" I told him where I was intending to go. Ray said, "Can you adjust those plans to meet me at U.S. Steel in Lorain? I have a meeting set up with some environmental engineers to demonstrate some dust control products."

"No problem," I answered and we made plans to meet later that morning at the steel mill.

To appreciate what happened at that meeting, I have to explain a little about the type work I did. My employer was Betz Laboratories. Betz is a specialty chemical company dealing in industrial water treatment and related products. We kept scale out of boilers and heat exchangers, silt and mud out of once through cooling systems, protected piping systems from corrosion, plus many other things. I worked for the Betz division that only dealt with large industrial customers. We didn't just sell chemicals. We had to oversee their application. We set up testing programs and trained the customer's employees in how to apply, monitor, and adjust the products they used. Customers were not obtained by a single sales call. They were obtained by a campaign. It took months, sometimes years, to gain a new client.

U.S. Steel in Lorain was already a customer of mine. I actually had four different accounts in that large plant. The environmental engineers we called on that day where not very familiar with the other work we did there. Ray and I put on a little demonstration of what we called dust control chemicals. When we finished I asked one of the young engineers what he thought.

"Interesting," the engineer said, "I think we'll try some."

"Great," I said. "How much would you like to try?"

Now I was expecting him to say a five gallon pail or maybe even a fifty five gallon drum. Ray and I were both shocked when he said, "Let's start with eight thousand gallons."

"Eight thousand gallons!" I said. "Do you have any idea how much that will cost?" When I said that, I think Ray could have killed me. It wasn't exactly what you want your salesman to say.

It was what the young engineer said next, that took my mind back to the night before. "I don't care what it will cost. I have to spend a million dollars and I'm having trouble spending it."

Suddenly a tingle went through my body. I knew what it was. It was the Holy Spirit letting me know that this was the confirmation that had been promised to me the night before. "THIS IS AS BAD AS IT IS GOING TO GET FOR YOU." Jesus had said. "SOMETHING WILL HAPPEN TOMORROW TO PROVE THAT EVERYTHING I SAY TONIGHT IS TRUE." This was that something! It was totally unplanned. I hadn't set up the meeting. I didn't even know what dust control chemicals were before that day. When a salesman hears a customer say that he doesn't care about cost and needs help spending a million dollars, that is not your everyday occurrence!

What makes this even more amazing is the ridiculous circumstances that surrounded the whole event. This large order, that literally came out of the blue in one day, was never repeated again. U.S. Steel actually ordered only six thousand gallons of the product because we could not get a big enough bulk chemical feed tank into the plant to hold eight thousand gallons. Nevertheless the order was for over $50,000 dollars. It proved to be just what I needed to secure my position with Betz. U.S. Steel purchased the product because the EPA had told them they had to spend a million dollars that year on fugitive emissions from the plant. They were ordered to spend the money to comply with new regulations. Shortly after they ordered the product, the economy in the steel industry got very bleak. U.S. Steel basically told the EPA to forget it. Money was simply not available any more to meet their mandate. This order had come out of nowhere, and to nowhere it returned, but it saved my career with Betz. I knew it was the confirmation of my miraculous conversation with God.

At the time this occurred in my life I was not attending church, and I was not actively seeking God. Sherryl and I had conversations about religion. Glenda had tried to get me to understand things from a Christian perspective, but basically I was just continuing along like I had been. I didn't have any idea why God would intervene on my behalf in the awesome way that he did. I didn't find out until over a year later, that on the Sunday that Jesus spoke to me, Glenda had asked for special prayer for me at her church that morning. Glenda sensed that I was in trouble. She asked her church family to intercede for me. Their prayer was definitely answered. That little country church was destined to play a major role in Sherryl's and my life.

If you think the experience I just related to you magically transformed me, then you are being overly optimistic. It did change me. I was now certain that God exists. How could I not be? After all, I actually heard Him! I wasn't, however, just going to automatically accept the authority of scripture or Christian doctrine. I was going to learn about it, examine it and see if it made sense. If it is the truth, then it should be logical. If it is true, then it should line up with what I observe. I was going to critically examine everything.

I began listening to Christian radio. I began reading the Bible. I began going to Church. I did not just accept what I heard or read. Instead I looked for reasons not to believe. What I learned is there are no reasons not to believe.

Christianity makes perfect sense. It is logical. It is the only plausible explanation for what I observe in the world.

After almost two years of listening, reading and going to church, I finally began to understand what the Bible means when it speaks of the unregenerate mind. I understand because I had one. Until the Holy Spirit is able to move on a person's heart, Christianity seems foolish to him.

The world has an opinion formed concerning Jesus and the Church that is not based on fact or logic. The opinion is based on misinformation and lies. Satan is a liar and the father of lies. That is how he works. Jesus is the Way, the Truth, and the Life. No matter how much the evidence, logic and observation supports the Truth (Jesus), the unregenerate mind can't accept it.

The world views fundamentalist Christians as brainwashed. It doesn't understand that we see ourselves as being recovered from brainwashing. I can give you an example that is easy to understand. Many who read this will automatically have a negative reaction to the word "fundamentalist." If you did, it is because you have been brainwashed into believing that fundamentalist means something that it doesn't.

Don't feel bad, because the computer program I am using to write this book has been brainwashed as well. When I go to the thesaurus in the computer, here are the words it provides for Fundamentalist: immovability, bitter-ender, reactionary, conservative, extremist, diehard, old liner, praetorian and pull back. I wasn't sure what praetorian meant so here is what the thesaurus said for it: dishonest, corrupt, sinister and able to be bribed. How many of those words have a good connotation to you? Not many, I think.

Now what does the word fundamental mean? Here is what the thesaurus has for the word fundamental: essential, key, basic, basal, crucial, central, bottom, axiomatic and chief. I wasn't positive what axiomatic meant so I checked it on the thesaurus. It means self evident, obvious and well known. How many of those words have a positive connotation? All of them do! How can fundamentals be good and a fundamentalist (one who believes the fundamentals) be bad? That is just one example of how the world doesn't think logically. It is easily tricked and lied to.

A fundamentalist Christian is the only kind of Christian there is. If you don't believe the essentials, the keys, the basics, the crucial, the self evident, then you don't believe! You are not a Christian. Within the liberal Christian subculture, people who view themselves as Christians often think "born again" Christians are fanatics. They see a fundamentalist Christian as being a negative thing to be. They are believing a lie. Jesus Himself said, "You must be born again." John 3:7. If you don't accept what Jesus said then you believe He is a liar. If Jesus is a liar, then He is not sinless. If Jesus is not sinless, then He is not the perfect sacrifice for our sins. This is fundamental!

People who call themselves Christians and don't believe the fundamentals are not thinking logically. They may be in for a rude awakening when they stand before God. None of us can tell who is saved and who is not. There is one thing I am sure of. I am not God. I am not going to pick and choose what parts of the Bible God got right, and have the audacity to tell Him were He made mistakes. I came away with one undeniable awareness from Jesus' brief conversation with me. He knows what He's doing. He doesn't make mistakes.

My brain was unwashed. My eyes were opened. My unregenerate mind suddenly was regenerated. I was blind but now I see. My sister Glenda had tried to explain it to me before, but she couldn't break through. If you are trying to reach someone with the saving knowledge of Jesus Christ and you are not bathing that person in prayer, the task may be impossible. Pray for the Holy Spirit to move on that person's heart. Prayer is the first resort, not the last resort.

When I was playing high school football, I played corner-back when on defense. All during my junior year the coach constantly reminded me to watch my keys. That meant to watch the player I was to defend and react to what he did. What that player did would tell me where the ball was. Although the coach continually reminded me, I never really believed that was the best way to do things. I found myself sneaking peaks at the quarterback and back at the ball.

When football season started my senior year, the coach continued to harp on the same thing. Watch your keys! Then one practice, like a light switch was suddenly turned on, I decided to listen to the coach and trust him. I watched my keys. I went from an average player to an outstanding player. I went from a couple of interceptions the year before to seven interceptions my senior year. My number of tackles nearly doubled.

In that personal example you see how the truth had always been made known to me, but I wasn't willing to accept it. The truth didn't change. I did. My football mind went from being unregenerate to regenerate, when I abandoned my own incorrect ways and accepted the fact that the coach knew a better way. In a nut shell, that is what happened in my life. Thank God!

The miracle of that evening was the turning point of my life, but people are not usually changed instantly. That was definitely true in my case. I would still have difficult times ahead and tears would still be shed, but I had a promise straight from the Lord himself, it would never be that bad again.

# Chapter Nine

# *It Does Get Better*

※

You can't hear the voice of God and not have things begin to change in your life. When you are absolutely sure that God does exist, and he loves you, you want to get to know him better. At least I did. I had a thirst to learn about God.

The excellent Christian ministries that I began listening to on the radio, the books Glenda recommended, and most of all the Bible, helped me handle the problems I still faced with my ex-wife and kids. The fire I began to exhibit for God, also helped to move my relationship forward with Sherryl.

It was early June of 1981. My divorce had become final in March. Sherryl and I had become friends the day after I moved to my parents' house. Actually our friendship had begun that night we met the year before. We saw each other often and dated regularly. She had encouraged me to date others. In fact she insisted on it. She continued to see others as well.

I never really enjoyed the whole dating scene. I was thirty

two years old. I had two children. I really wanted to be happily married, if such a thing was possible. Sherryl, on the other hand, had adapted well to the single life. She seemed to enjoy her independence. It wasn't that she didn't want to be married again. She did. She was just afraid of making another mistake. Looking back, I can't help but think it was God's plan that kept the beautiful twenty eight year old blonde available for me.

Sherryl would talk to me with complete candor. She told me that I didn't really fit the picture she had in her mind of the perfect husband. I wasn't tall, dark and handsome. Actually, she said I was handsome enough, but I wasn't hairy enough. I'm just under 5'10" and my reddish blonde hair, fair skin and hairless chest differed from what her mind had fashioned as her spouse. Even with these short comings, we grew closer and closer.

Sherryl began to realize the magnitude of the miraculous event that had occurred in my life when she saw the changes it brought about in me. Earlier I mentioned how Sherryl and I liked the movie "When Harry Met Sally." In the movie Harry and Sally knew each other for years. They became best friends before they eventually got married. Sherryl has a plaque that says "Happiness is marrying your best friend." We really believe that. Realizing that is not always as simple as it sounds. It took Harry and Sally twelve years in the movie. It took Sherryl and I less than a year, but there were bumps in the road.

Prior to God's intervention, when He spoke to me, neither Sherryl nor I were complying with the Lord's morality. In the movie, Harry tells Sally how a man wants to leave right after having relations with a woman that he doesn't love. I found that to be true. I regret to say that in the few such experiences I had in my life, I always had the same thought go through my mind. "Why had this been so important to me?" I would think to myself. It was never important to me after it happened. I always regretted the experience. The world says sex without commitment is where it's at. The world says that it is a good thing. That is a lie. Instead of that type of sex making me happy, it made me feel empty. Some of the saddest and most pathetic people in the world are the ones who have believed that lie.

During the first six months after I knew my marriage was over, I no longer had to try an be faithful to anyone. The lies Satan feeds us, tell us that is a good thing. I never found it to be good. I only found it to be sad. Sherryl was the one person I was with that I never wanted to leave. She was important to me. I knew why. I loved her.

One thing I must stress. Love is not an emotion based on feelings. Love is never the result of runaway hormones. Feelings are a basis for lust, not love. Feelings are what the immature confuse with love.

Love is a decision. It is a conscious decision to commit yourself to the well being of another. True love means that you will place the well-being of the one you love above your own. Selfishness prevents true love.

I never would have divorced my first wife, if she had given me any indication that she was capable of committing to our relationship. The same is true of Sherryl and her first husband. Our spouses were never willing to commit to either of us.

Immature people who live on feelings are pawns in Satan's hands. Instead of human beings created in God's image, they reduce themselves to the level of animals controlled by hormones. Think of the untold misery that Satan causes when he uses people who are controlled by their feelings. Feelings are foundationless.

Miserable immature spouses go from marriage to marriage looking for someone to make them happy. I loved Sherryl because I knew she was a person who didn't need anyone else to make her happy. Her happiness came from within, not from without. She was a mature person. She had a firm foundation.

I thought about marrying Sherryl almost right from that first conversation after I had left home for good, but I didn't want to admit it to myself. I also knew that I couldn't let her know. I sensed that if I tried to cling to her too quickly, it would only be bad for our relationship. I didn't want to make another mistake and I needed to give myself time. I had targeted my first wife the first time I met her. That had been a goal I regretted achieving. Sherryl and I were both older now, and we had learned from our experiences.

Sherryl actually insisted I date some other women. She was afraid that I was just attracted to her while I was on the rebound from my failed marriage. Although she didn't date much after we started seeing each other, she made it clear that she still could, and she did a little. She was a friend and it was for the best that we kept things that way.

The time I had as a bachelor made me realize I didn't like it. I liked being with Sherryl and I knew it. The evenings I spent dating others were almost like a forced duty, but it was good that I did it. I learned not to be possessive. I learned not to be jealous. I also learned how to begin to trust someone again.

The most important thing I learned was about myself. After my encounter with God, I realized that I was accountable for the decisions I made. A couple of weeks before that encounter, I had gone out with a woman that I knew from work. We had known each other for a few years and now we were both unattached adults. I knew I cared about Sherryl, but she was actually insisting that I see other women. The world's message to me was that this was an ideal situation. The girl was a nice young lady and we had been casual friends for some time through our jobs. Now that I was divorced, and Sherryl was telling me to see other women, this girl seemed to be a natural choice to ask out. Behaving like the world expected us to, we had an intimate physical encounter. Before I left that evening we scheduled a second date. Before that second date arrived, God did. My encounter with the Lord occurred.

It had only been a few days since God's voice had kept me from driving into that tree. I didn't have much time to learn a lot about Him, but I had learned the most important things. He actually exists and He knows me. On my way over to fulfill my date with this young lady, I hadn't realized how that knowledge had already changed me.

When I got to the woman's house I knew she was anticipating the same type of evening we had before. To be honest, so was I, until I actually arrived there. Instead of an intimate physical encounter, I witnessed to her. I told her about the miracle conversation I had with the Lord. I told her about Sherryl and that I loved her. Then I told her that I realized something I needed to prove to myself. I had eventually been unfaithful in a miserable marriage. I felt that I had been justified because of all the times my ex-wife had been unfaithful to me. Now, I needed to know that I could be faithful to Sherryl, even though we weren't married, engaged, or even seeing each other exclusively. If I could be faithful now, I knew I always would be, if we ever were to get married. It was also a concession to begin accepting God's morality and abandoning my own.

I don't want to mislead anyone into thinking that I suddenly became so self controlled that I became celibate. Sherryl and I had been friends, but we had also been lovers. I think we both knew we loved each other very early in our relationship. Even so, we knew we needed time to learn more about each other than just what we had physically together.

It was kind of amazing that our former spouses seemed so discontent that they sought other physical relationships. Sherryl and I both had been very disappointed in that aspect of our first marriages. From the beginning the physical relationship Sherryl and I shared was, and always has been, wonderful. Although we hadn't reached God's moral standard I knew one thing now. I loved Sherryl. I would be faithful to her alone. I would try to win her hand in marriage. I purchased an engagement ring. It was a good thing I kept the receipt!

It was the very end of June or early July and Sherryl had made plans to go to Ocean City, New Jersey with Nancy. Nancy was another nurse at the hospital where Sherryl worked. The two girls had a lot in common. Nancy was the head nurse in the intensive care unit. Sherryl was the head nurse in the coronary care unit. Both were pretty blondes. Both had sons named Chad that were about the same age. Both had just gone through a divorce. They quickly became great friends. Their friendship had seen them through the previous two years. Now, I came along. Sherryl and I started spending more time together than Nancy and Sherryl did. I think this frightened Sherryl a little. She didn't want to lose the close ties she and Nancy had. At the same time Nancy started getting pretty serious with a male friend of her own. The two girls decided it was time to get away together again and renew old bonds.

Sherryl was looking forward to the time with her friend. It would be nice to get away from any male influences for a while. She didn't know that Nancy wasn't planning to completely leave out the male that was influencing her.

Nancy called me and told me that the guy she was seeing wanted, to join her in Ocean City at the end of the week. She knew this would leave Sherryl all alone, unless I could get away and join her about the same time. I told Nancy that I could. I also told her I was thinking about proposing to Sherryl. I asked Nancy if she thought Sherryl would accept. She said she thought she would.

Nancy thought it would be nice if my showing up was a surprise. That seemed like a good idea to me. I just wanted to be with Sherryl. Looking back on it, surprising Sherryl probably wasn't a good idea. She was glad to see me, especially when Nancy had her boyfriend show up, but I think she was a little annoyed with Nancy. I think Sherryl really wanted the time to be with her. It hurt her a little that Nancy valued the time with her boyfriend more than their time together.

After I arrived, Sherryl and I bought tickets to see Wayne Newton in Atlantic City. After dinner and the show, sitting there at our table, I asked Sherryl to marry me. She said no. Not quite that bluntly. She was very nice about it. She didn't want to hurt me, but it was no just the same.

That proved to be a difficult evening for both of us. We got away from the crowds and back to my car, where we could just sit and talk. Remember, Sherryl likes to talk. Well we talked and we cried. I was a little surprised that she said no. I told her that I was accustomed to getting what I wanted, and that I wanted to marry her. I told her that I thought she loved me, and that we belonged together.

Sherryl told me that it was too soon after my divorce. She said I needed more time to be sure I knew what I wanted. Most of all, she told me, she was scared. She didn't want to make a mistake again. She never expected to be divorced the first time. She surely didn't want it to happen again. There was one other factor that she was totally honest about. It was my vasectomy.

Sherryl had just turned twenty nine. She wanted to have more children. Like always we could talk about everything, openly and honestly. Every point she made was a valid one. It just made me respect and love her even more. We decided that we would just continue with things the way they were. I would return the engagement ring. I told her that would be an embarrassing experience that I wasn't going to risk having again. I said that if we were ever going to get married, she would have to ask me the next time. She understood.

The next few weeks were a little bumpy. Sherryl was scared and she pulled away a little. She actually lied to me once for a couple of days, when she went out with someone else. Her doing it wasn't the problem, her being afraid to tell me about it was. That almost broke us up, but we survived it.

I was learning a lot about the Lord. I think everyone that knew me probably thought that Sherryl was influencing me towards my Christian walk. The truth was I was actually the one moving Sherryl back to the Lord. This spiritual aspect was the final piece of the puzzle that was needed to cement our lives together.

I remember after my conversation with God, I started praying again. Every evening I was praying that God would have Sherryl marry me. But I was learning quickly. It dawned on me that what I was praying for was wrong. Praying like that is almost like trying to practice witchcraft. I had no right to ask God to manipulate Sherryl or anyone else. My prayers changed. I decided to trust God. I would pray like this. "Lord, I love Sherryl and I think she would be a wonderful wife for me. I know you love me and want what is best for me. If Sherryl isn't the woman I should share my life with, then I know who you have in mind will be wonderful, because I can't imagine anyone being better for me than Sher. Whoever you have in mind for me, let me honor her and be a godly husband."

By late July of 1981, I decided to see a doctor about having my vasectomy reversed. It had been five years since I had it done. The odds for a successful reversal were not high. I went to the Cleveland Clinic because they represented the best chance I had for success. I knew that Sherryl wanted to have more children and so did I. Even if Sherryl was never to be my wife, I was only thirty three and with all the problems I was having seeing my children, I knew I wanted more children as well. What made the decision difficult was that it was elective surgery. It wasn't covered by my hospitalization. It was going to cost five thousand dollars and there was a good chance it wouldn't work. I decided it was worth the risk.

I had the surgery done. It was one of those adventures in my life that I would have rather avoided. The follow up appointment did not give me the results I hoped for. Sherryl and I both remember how the doctor put it to us. "Your count is low and slow." The Doctor said. Basically it meant the odds were quite small that I would ever father another child. When Sherryl and I got the news I wasn't sure if it meant that my chances of ever marrying Sher were gone. I knew how much she wanted at least one more child. I could understand if that kept her from marrying me.

What made the whole thing even harder for me to accept was the fact that my ex-wife was pregnant. I had the vasectomy because of her abortion. She supposedly couldn't have children because of the medication she was taking. Now she was already having a child. She would go on to have several more.

The doctor who had performed the vasectomy had warned me about this very scenario. I wished I had listened. I hoped it wouldn't keep me from the woman I loved.

# Chapter Ten

# *She Asks Me!*

*A* rock group called "The Who" had a song in the late 60's with lyrics that said, "that deaf, dumb and blind kid." Those lyrics remind me of myself. I had lived thirty three years and had been deaf when it came to hearing God. I always let myself drown Him out. I had been dumb, not in the sense of being unable to talk, but in respect to being dumb as in stupid. I had been blind in never being able to see that God was there all the time.

Like a loving parent, God let me make mistakes. He didn't want to see me hurt. I understood that now, because I knew He hurt more for me than I did. He had to stand by and let the pain teach me. He had to wait to see if I would ever share control of my life with Him. We are not made to be puppets or robots. We are made in the image of God to have free will. If God's purpose for us is to control us, He can accomplish that any time He chooses. I believe his purpose for us is fellowship.

I don't pretend to be a theologian. I know that I don't have answers to all the tough questions. I realize more with each passing day that God and his purposes are not within my comprehension. I think up my own theories about Him. I try to explain why things are the way they are. Most of us do that all the time. We want to figure Him out. We want to know all His plans. We want to corner the market on understanding God. We all want to be able to put Him in a box, label Him, and file Him away for when we really need Him.

As I read my Bible, I began to realize that I had always wanted God to be my cosmic butler in the sky. A servant who's only job was to spoil me rotten. I wanted Him to be a mixture of Superman, Bill Gates, and a genie. I wanted Him to accept that I ignored Him completely until I needed something. I realized I wanted to be god and I wanted God to be my servant.

I think the job that most people want God to fill would be the worst position in creation. Many want God to provide for their every need. We want Him to wait on us hand and foot. We want to be wet nursed for eternity. Would you want that job? I am pretty sure God doesn't want it either.

When Jesus spoke to me I realized that He was a being very much like me. A family is God's best example for us to begin to comprehend what eternity has in store. Think about how a healthy family gives us a glimpse of Godly love. Parents love, protect, instruct, and provide for their children. The children are created by the parents. They are formed in the parents' image, but they are unique and separate individuals. Parents are supposed to be two individuals who have become one flesh. That intimate relationship is the one God chose to use as the illustration of what He wants our relationship with him to be like. We are to be the bride of Christ. The family as God intends it to be is a living organism that depends on love. I believe it is a tiny taste of heaven. It's an idea I will revisit later in our story.

In June, Sherryl sang for her sister Debbie's wedding.

Deb and her husband Ben were very active members in the Assembly of God Church in Wellington that Sherryl had attended. Being back in her home church singing for the wedding, provided the first impetus for Sherryl to want to return to church.

I attended the wedding. Finding a church to attend was now a priority on my list as well. Sherryl and I started going to church together. We attended the Assembly of God and we also attended my sister Glenda's church. I enjoyed church at either place, but I felt more comfortable at the little country church in Penfield where Glenda and my parents were attending. Glenda was the music director. She quickly latched on to Sherryl and her talent.

At that time the church at Penfield was a United Church of Christ. The minister was a retired Navy chaplain named Bill Rugg. Bill and his wife Mary were wonderful Christians. Bill had been the minister at the First Baptist Church in Wellington, but a theological split occurred and Bill resigned. Pastor Rugg's navy pension allowed him to fill the ministerial vacancy that existed at the Penfield United Church of Christ for a very tiny salary. A tiny salary was all that the church could afford.

I may be guilty of seeing miracles and God's hand in more things than other people would, but I can't help thinking that God placed Bill and Mary right where He needed them. When Bill became the pastor at Penfield, the church had only a few core families. Bill brought a few more people with him from the Baptist church. One of those people was my sister Glenda. Just a few years earlier the church at Penfield almost went out of existence. Under Bill and Mary's leadership and commitment to the fundamentals of the Christian faith, the church developed a solid congregation.

Things were changing in my life. Most of the changes were very good. Sherryl and I grew closer and closer. We were growing closer to the Lord as well. I still had one problem. I hadn't learned to cope with my ex-wife. She continued to emotionally manipulate my children and through them, me.

Friend is a word that we use a lot. It is a label that we place on many people. The truth is most of those we call our friends are really just acquaintances. A friend is someone you can depend on. A best friend is someone you go to when you need support.

I had another terrible time trying to get my kids for a visitation. My ex-wife had pulled all the right strings to torment me again. I wasn't suicidal like I had been a couple of months earlier, but I was wallowing in self-pity again. I felt like I needed a loving shoulder to cry on. I needed someone to share my pain. I drove over to Sherryl's house.

When I got to Sherryl's, I had tears running down my face. I was a forlorn character looking for that understanding shoulder. I knocked on her door. Seconds later that wonderful girl opened the door and saw my sorrowful form standing there. "Sherryl, she (my ex-wife) is driving me crazy!" I said. I waited for the door to swing open and beckon me in. I didn't get what I expected.

"She's driving you crazy because you let her drive you crazy." Sherryl said. Then she closed the door.

I stood there for a moment. I was trying to figure out what had just happened. This didn't follow the script I had written in my mind. There was no shoulder! There was no sharing my pain! There wasn't even talk! She always wanted to talk! I didn't know what to do.

Finally, I turned around and went back to my car. I was starting to get angry. I thought she cared about me! I started to drive the mile that took me to my parents' house. As I made the short trip home I began to replay what I had just heard.

I work in sales. It is important to be a good listener when you're in sales. I always tell Sherryl there is a big difference between hearing and listening. I had heard what Sherryl said but I hadn't listened to her. Now, I began to listen to what she had said. My resentment for her seeming lack of concern began to transform into gratitude for her blunt wisdom. Her comment deserved some examination.

Once I got home I mulled over what Sherryl had said. "She drives you crazy because you let her drive you crazy." Then she shuts the door. It was harsh but effective. I got the point.

I began to understand that I couldn't control what my ex-wife did. The only thing I had control over was how I reacted to it. She only had power over me because I allowed her to have it.

You would think something so obvious would be understood by everyone. Sadly, most people never grasp that simple truth. I didn't like what my ex-wife was doing but I had no power to change it. I could only control what I did and how I reacted. Until I realized that fact, I simply granted her authority over my life that she could only have with my approval. My best friend helped me learn an important lesson.

A true friend cares enough to tell you the truth. Sherryl cared enough to avoid the obvious reaction and replace it with a punch of reality. It was a point she probably had tried to make in a more subtle way before, and I had been too dense to grasp it. Sherryl did what best friends are supposed to do. She confronted me when I needed it, instead of comforting me because I wanted it. Friends who care enough to tell you the truth, are friends indeed.

The lesson I had just learned has a spiritual application as well. We can't control what Satan does. He is a liar and he wants to harm us. We can't control him but we can control how we react to him. We are accountable for how we deal with Satan's lies. Satan has power over us only when we give it to him. Why would anyone give him power? We do it because we believe a lie. We are all guilty of it. Satan is very good at lying. Christians show they are maturing as they get better and better at recognizing the Devil's lies. The Devil has many very basic lies that most of our culture has accepted. Some examples are:

1. Dirty is funny.
2. Abortion is choice.
3. Happiness depends on circumstances.
4. Wealth means security.
5. Evolution is fact.
6. God is dead.
7. Jesus isn't the only way.
8. Absolute truth does not exist.
9. The Bible contradicts itself.

The list can go on for pages. Think for a few moments and discover the lies you have given power over you. Maybe its pornography, drugs, sex, alcohol, dishonesty, greed, selfishness, or depression. It could be almost anything. But you don't have to give it power. You are responsible. Responsibility is the price of free will .

Sherryl and I continued to grow closer and closer. Our relationship left nothing to be desired as far as I was concerned. I loved Sherryl. My parents loved Sherryl. My kids loved Sherryl, even though they couldn't admit to it. I loved her family and they all seemed happy with me. I was ready to tie the knot, but I had to wait for Sherryl to ask me.

Glenda and I had a few conversations concerning my love life. She offered me some advice. "Don't let Sherryl be too comfortable with the idea you will always be waiting for her." Glenda said. "If she feels too sure of you, it could be a long time before she ever asks you to marry her. Maybe you need to do something that might make her a little uneasy." It was a point well made.

One of the things I liked most about the relationship

Sherryl and I had, was the fact that we were honest with each other. There wasn't any need for all the games people often play. Even so, sometimes some strategy is required in the human drama we call courtship.

In my life I have done many stupid things, but the strategy I came up with to get Sherryl to finally ask me to marry her, bordered on shear genius, if I do say so myself.

Actually, I didn't come up with any strategy at all. What happened was far too effective for me to have thought it up. I can't even remember the circumstances surrounding how it occurred. I think it was another case of divine intervention. To this day I doubt that Sherryl will admit what motivated her to finally ask me to marry her. I think I know what it was.

Have I got you wondering? What do you think would have prompted Sherryl to lose her fear of making another mistake and finally decide she was ready to marry me? Who was the one person that Sherryl might think I could really gain an interest in? If you thought my ex-wife you're way off. That would have only convinced Sherryl that I wasn't very bright. It was Nancy.

Nancy was Sherryl's best friend, besides me. There were many things about Nancy that Sherryl loved. Since that trip to Ocean City, things had not gone as smoothly between Nancy and her boy friend as they had between Sherryl and me. Even though Sherryl had turned down my proposal, our relationship had only continued to grow stronger.

Nancy's relationship hadn't gone quite as well. I can't even recall the circumstances, but one night in September of 1981 I ran into Nancy. It may have been at the Mall. I don't remember. I wasn't with Sherryl that night and I don't know why. She may have been working or she may have accepted a date with someone else. I just can't remember. Anyway, Nancy and I both wanted to talk over what was going on in our relationships. I ended up going over to Nancy's house and we sat at her kitchen table and discussed our situations.

Nancy and I both loved Sherryl, so it was easy for her to offer help and give me insight in how I might finally get Sherryl to commit to me. I didn't know the man Nancy was seeing that well. We had double dated with them a few times and that was the extent of my knowledge of the guy. I gave her a male's point of view on a few questions she had.

We also talked about God. I remember witnessing to her about the need for the Lord to be involved in people's lives. I told her I thought it was very difficult for marriages without a spiritual foundation to succeed. We talked for quite a while before we realized that it was very late.

When I followed Nancy to her house, my car was very low on gas. I hadn't told her I needed to stop at a gas station before we left, and I had no way of signaling her that I needed to stop for fuel. Since I wasn't sure I could find her house, I just continued until we got there. I really didn't think I would be there very long, but now the conversation had lasted until past midnight. All the nearby gas stations were closed. Nancy's two boys were there with us and she had a spare bedroom. She insisted I just stay there overnight rather than risk running out of gas trying to find an opened station. Since I knew the nearest all-night station was miles away, and I wasn't sure I could make it there, I thought it was a good idea to wait till morning.

I think it was probably God's idea. It was all perfectly innocent. I told Sherryl all about it. Guess what, Sherryl asked me to marry her a few days later. I don't know if Sherryl will admit it or not, but I think that night at Nancy's made her a little less positive that she could continue to postpone a decision.

Sherryl knew that nothing happened between Nancy and me. She also knew Nancy. Sherryl loved Nancy. I think in the back of her mind she may have felt that since she liked Nancy so much, maybe I could become interested in her. I know that Nancy had told Sherryl that she thought I was a nice man and would make a good husband. Now, I wasn't interested in Nancy, and she wasn't interested in me. Sherryl knew that. She also knew I loved her, but I do think that evening made her decide not to take any chances. I was her man and she was going to stake her claim. She asked me to marry her. I said "NO!" Just kidding! Of course I said yes.

"See, I told you I always get what I want." I told Sherryl. Sometimes I had wanted the wrong thing. Sometimes what I desired had not been good for me. Not this time. God had given me my heart's desire. God had answered my prayers.

# Chapter Eleven

# The Wedding

※

*I*t had been ten months since I moved out of my home when I knew that my marriage was unsalvageable. In those ten months my life had changed dramatically. I found new personal happiness I had never known before as an adult. I also experienced deep pain over the loss of daily contact with my two children. I had rediscovered my Savior. It was a jammed packed ten months of my life. It was only a hint of what was to come.

During those months I was making house payments on the home that Sherryl's former husband had built for my ex-wife and me. My wife married the man with the background of felony convictions before the end of June in 1981. She already had a child by the time Sherryl and I decided to get married in late September.

My children's new step father was back in trouble with the law. He needed money for legal fees. Through my attorney's efforts I received credit for ten months of house payments. Those payments lowered my former wife's equity in the home. This made it possible for me to buy my house back from her at a cost that I could afford. I regained my home with a quit claim deed. I moved back into my house by the end of October in 1981. That was a happy day for my parents and me.

When Sherryl was married the first time, she had a very large wedding. When I got married the first time, I had eloped. I was so proud of Sherryl and so happy with the way my life was changing that I wanted to celebrate it with family and friends. I wanted to have a wedding. I wanted to be married in church. We were going to have to pay for it ourselves, but Sherryl liked the idea as well. We began to start planning.

I am a romantic, but I am a practical romantic. I wanted a nice wedding and I also wanted a great honeymoon. Like most people, money was not an unlimited resource. To achieve our goals we had to think things through and make some wise decisions.

We both decided that a honeymoon cruise would be perfect. We started to shop around for an affordable deal on a seven day Caribbean cruise. We found what we wanted and booked it. It was to leave on January 1st , 1982. That was perfect because we planned our Wedding to fall between Christmas and New Years. We picked that time because Sherryl's brother Ron and his family would be home for Christmas from California.

Sherryl was a registered nurse and she earned a good income. I worked for Betz Laboratories and had a nice income as well. We were far from rich, but together we made a decent living. I had heard about the marriage penalty in the tax code. I decided it would be a good idea to check on what our marriage might do to our income tax obligation.

The news was not good. If we married before the end of the year we were going to owe more than $2,400 in additional income taxes. The need to raise extra money to pay

Uncle Sam was going to cost us our honeymoon. That was a cost we weren't willing to pay.

Our wedding was going to have to be at an unusual time. We couldn't be married until after midnight on New Years Eve. We would make our reception everyone's New Year's Eve celebration. Sherryl thought it was a neat idea and so did I. We had 2,400 reasons to like the idea. I am sure that our family and friends didn't like the idea as much as we did. They didn't have the same incentive. For purely practical reasons, that became our plan.

Sherryl wanted to be married in the Assembly of God Church she had attended. We made an appointment and met with the pastor. He was very nice but he said he would have to discuss it with the church board. When we came back for another meeting he apologized and said he couldn't marry us. The pastor was in a very difficult situation. I completely understood.

Sherryl had been a very active member in the church. Her first husband had become a board member. His infidelity had not been good for the church. Some members felt Sherryl was wrong to divorce him because he indicated that he wanted to stay married. The problem was that Sherryl knew he didn't want to stay faithful. The whole situation made many people uncomfortable. The current church board was concerned about opening up old wounds. Sherryl was a little hurt by it, but she understood.

When we look back on it, we see the Lord's hand in the whole thing. We both think that God wanted us to attend the little church in Penfield. The whole situation was also a good lesson for both of us about church discipline. The true Church is supposed to exercise discipline. It is responsible for holding the line in an effort to keep God's holy standards. The Church must also show the grace of God and His forgiveness. It is a difficult balance to maintain. We appreciate how tough a challenge it is.

I view the Bible as a book that stresses balance. More than any other book I know of, it lays before the reader the frailties and failures of its heroes. Why? I think it does it to show how easily we humans can get out of balance. We tend to overemphasize one area, while we under value another. It was not the Romans who sought to kill Jesus. It was the religious leaders of the Jews. Why? Because they were out of balance. They had information about God, but they lacked fellowship and intimacy with Him. It is a struggle that we all face daily. We are all out of balance to some degree. When we really get in trouble and are struggling the most, it is because we are way out of balance.

What would happen if Jesus began attending your church? Our first reaction is that everyone would be very happy about it. We assume we would recognize Him right away. Unfortunately, that probably would not be the case. Jesus would upset many people because He would bring people into the church that some folks wouldn't like. Bikers, drug addicts, prostitutes, even IRS agents would be welcomed into the flock. He would make many uncomfortable because He so easily loved and accepted people. Jesus would upset others because He would remind them of their own failures and hidden prejudices. Jesus would not fit into the box that everyone had fashioned for God. The truth is your church would probably gain many new members and lose many old ones. This would most likely happen in every church in the world. The question is, would you be one who stayed or one who left? Think about it.

Sherryl and I met with Reverend Rugg. He agreed to marry us and to do it right after midnight on New Year's Eve. We had already attended Penfield Church a few times, but now we became committed to the church. It became our church. I was thirty three years old, and for the first time in my life, I had a church home. I had a church family. It was wonderful.

The church at Penfield, in many ways, was a mirror of our

lives. It had a long history. Originally it was a strong, fundamentally sound, Christian Church. Then it had problems with pastors and a denomination that continually became more and more liberal. Those problems caused it to weaken in numbers and distance itself from God's word. Years without direction almost cost the church its existence, but the Lord was still hanging on to it. He provided a few families who were committed to seeing it survive. They saw their diligence rewarded when God provided Pastor Bill Rugg. When Sherryl and I started attending the church it was in a position similar to mine. It was changing, growing, and learning. Church should always be changing, growing and learning. Just like all of us. I like a saying I heard once on a sales training tape. "When you're green, you grow. When you're ripe, you rot."

I was new in my Christian walk. Sherryl and I did some things during this time in our lives that we wouldn't do today and that we definitely would not recommend. These things could have been a bad witness and a stumbling block to some. I am sure that they made Pastor Rugg and some of our church family uneasy. We regret that, but we also are thankful for the patience and love that our new church family showed to us. They loved us even when we were a little hard to take. So does Jesus. Praise the Lord!

One of the things we did, for purely practical reasons, was have Sherryl move into my home a few days before the wedding. We had found a renter for Sherryl's half of the duplex she owned. We needed to get Sherryl moved out and that situation taken care of before we left for the honeymoon. Even though it made practical sense, it was not a good witness to others.

Another thing we did, that we wouldn't do now, was have alcohol at the reception. It was News Year's Eve and some of Sherryl's and my coworkers may not have attended if alcohol was not provided. God blessed us by not allowing the alcohol to harm anyone, but it is something that we would not risk today. It was not a good witness to some who attended. Unfortunately, many people may not have attended if we hadn't allowed alcoholic beverages. That is because many have bought one of Satan's lies. They think that alcohol is necessary to have a good time.

I don't take the theological position that a person should never drink any alcohol. I think that position may be a little out of balance with the entirety of scripture. We are not bound by legalism. I just think that we were a little insensitive to some of our Christian brothers and sisters who preferred that alcohol not be present. I think at the same time we were too willing to cave into pressures from others who expected and wanted alcohol to be available. We couldn't please everyone, and we didn't.

Even with these concerns the wedding turned out to be a great night. My two children didn't get to attend. Their mother had successfully ruined that part of the evening, but Sherryl's son Chad was part of the ceremony.

We had music begin about twenty minutes before midnight. We probably overdid the music a little. Altogether there were seventeen songs during the entire service. Most were done to take up time to get us past midnight. We needed to be sure we didn't actually get married before the new year had arrived. With my sister Glenda being the music director at the church and Sherryl's sister Debbie being an excellent singer, Sherryl had to be sure to show them off to everyone.

Glenda had been encouraging me to start singing. I did start singing in the choir, but she was also telling me I could sing solos. Since I was paying for this wedding, I decided I could sing in it if I wanted to. Being the hopeless romantic that I am, I wrote a song for Sherryl. I sang it to her during the service. She sang a song to me as well. After we were pronounced husband and wife, we sang a duet. That was the first time in my life I had ever sung a solo in public. Things were certainly changing.

The reception lasted until about 3:30 in the morning. I think everyone had a pretty good time. I remember when Sherryl threw the bridal bouquet. Nancy charged after it. She slipped and fell on the floor in her effort to get it. No wonder my talking to Nancy got Sherryl to ask me to marry her. It looked like Nancy really wanted to get married!

As the reception was nearing its conclusion, my new brothers in law cornered me. They had me drink a few toasts to my new lot in life. I don't remember much after that. I think that is why I wouldn't have alcohol at the reception if I could do it all over again. They drove us to the Sheraton Hotel at the airport in Cleveland. We got to bed about 4:30 am. We had a flight that left at 8:30 am. We almost missed it!

It had been a long and exhausting day and night. We were both tired. Now we were married. We were beginning a new life. It was going to be different and better than even we realized at that moment. We were together. We had both married our best friend in the whole world. We were ONE.

# Chapter Twelve

# A Whole New World

*T*he toasts at the end of our reception had made me totally useless to Sherryl for the remainder of the night. We were driven to the hotel and we managed to get ourselves, and our luggage, into the room. We made sure that we would get a wake up call in the morning and we went right to sleep. We probably kissed good night, but we were both so tired that we can't remember.

Neither Sherryl nor I are morning people. That morning of January 1st, 1982, our engines just didn't want to start. I don't know how long the phone rang trying to wake us up, but by the time we both finally came to our senses enough to realize where we were, we had to move quickly. We had a plane to catch! Somehow, by the grace of God, we just made our flight. It wasn't until we got to our seats in the plane and settled down that we finally had a chance to even look at each other. I remember sitting there and looking at this beautiful young woman. She was a gift from God. We were going on the trip of a lifetime, with our best friend. It was our honeymoon. It just doesn't get any better than that.

Now that we were awake, even though we were both still very tired, there was no thought of sleeping during the flight to Fort Lauderdale, FL. We had a chance to sit and talk. We went over everything that happened the night before. It had been different, but it was a good wedding. I knew without a doubt that we would have a good marriage. Sherryl would never be unfaithful and I would never be untrue to her. We not only loved and lusted for each other, we liked each other. We liked each other so much that we both enjoyed making the other person happy. Like everyone, we each had our own selfish desires, but we cared and respected each other so much that it was always easy to adjust to make our partner happy.

If you haven't figured it out yet, I really love and respect Sherryl. She is the most unselfish and giving person I have ever known. She would have to face many tough crises in the next few years. How she has handled them has only made me love her more every day. She is not perfect. We both have our little quirks and traits that bug the other, but in all the things that really matter, she gets an A+.

Selfishness and being self-centered are the cause of death for most relationships. I had spent my adult life trying to please a woman who wouldn't be pleased. Happiness is not dependent on circumstances or things. Happiness is a choice we make. I wanted to be happy in my first marriage, but marriage is meant to be a union. Two people become one in a marriage. Spouses that depend on their partners to fulfill their needs and make them happy, doom their relationship in two ways. First, they never learn to give. They are so concerned about their needs, that they never have the joy that comes from fulfilling the needs of their partner. Second, they never learn to be satisfied or content. They are always looking for external sources of fulfillment. If you are in an unhappy marriage, become unselfish. Stop thinking about yourself and focus on your mate. You may find that, if you make that change, your spouse may change for the better as well. Remember, you can't control what others do. You can only control how you respond.

All marriages have conflict. The difference between a good marriage and a bad one, is the way each partner handles conflict when it occurs. The more a marriage partner focuses on the faults of their spouse, the more selfish they become. Everything begins to center on what the other partner must do to make you happy. This is a road to ruin. Unless both partners begin to learn to focus on their mate, and do what they can to meet their mate's needs, divorce or unhappiness will result.

Marriage, as God intends it, is not dependent on your finding the perfect mate. It is dependent on your trying to be the perfect mate. I know that none of us are perfect, but if we place our effort into being the best mate we can be, we will usually find that we will gain a wonderful mate in return.

Marriage problems are not solved by divorce. God hates divorce. Changing your mate and not changing yourself will generally only increase your problems. Sherryl and I both realize that sometimes a marriage can't survive. That is never what God desires. God does understand though, and He can help you to understand yourself better. Learn from the mistakes you've made and let God in.

I wish that my first marriage could have been successful. Eventually, I had to admit it was never going to improve. That didn't make the Lord happy, but He does understand. He didn't forsake me for my failures. He had to endure the pain I caused Him with my own heartaches. He used that heartache to bring me closer to Him. He didn't leave me. He blessed me with a another one of His children. Sherryl was my second chance. We had both matured enough to learn what was really important in a mate. We would be happy because we wanted to make each other happy.

In the years ahead, when I had the opportunity to give my testimony, I would often relate a true story that happened to me years earlier. I was at the service department of a car dealership having a repair done on my company car. A woman pulled up in a brand new station wagon. When she got out of her car the service manager gave her a friendly welcome. It was apparent that the service manager knew the woman from previous service calls.

"What can I do for you Mrs. (whoever she was)?" The service manager asked.

"I want a new car!" came the woman's terse reply. "I'm sick and tired of this car! I am always having to bring it back in here for something. This is the third time! I want a new car! I've had it!" The woman's tone of voice and anger level shocked me.

"What seems to be the problem?" The service manager asked her in a remarkably calm reply.

"The radio doesn't work! A brand new car and the radio doesn't work! I want a new car. I'm sick of it!" the woman said, her voice showing more anger with every sentence. "Look, I turn it on and push the buttons and nothing! I want a new car!" she continued.

"Mrs. (whoever she was), did you set the stations?" the service manager asked her, again showing remarkable restraint.

"What do you mean, set the stations? I turn it on and push the buttons. That's all I've ever done. It doesn't work. I want a new car!" the woman said.

"Mrs. (?) did you read your owner's manual?" the service manager asked her.

"I haven't got time to read the owner's manual!" the lady shouted back. She was madder than ever. "I want a new car!"

"Mrs. (Jerk), there is nothing wrong with your radio. You simply have to set the stations on the buttons so that when you push them they are tuned to the stations you want." the service manager calmly explained to her. "I'll do it for you and show you how. Listen and tell me what stations you want the buttons to take you to. There is nothing wrong with the radio or your car. You just need to read your owner's manual so that you understand how it works."

The service manager's calm reply's finally quieted the woman. She got in the car and together they set the radio stations on her buttons.

That experience never left my memory. The lady was so angry and loud. The service manager was so calm and respectful. The woman made a complete fool of herself because she never bothered to read her owner's manual.

Years later, after all the experiences I had in my life, the meaning of that encounter became clear to me.

Most of us (including me) are just like that woman. We complain that something is wrong with the equipment or the manufacturer of our life. The problem is that we've never read the owner's manual. The Bible is the owner's manual for people. It has been provided by the manufacturer. It explains to us how everything works. We all tend to be just like that woman. We say "I haven't got time to read the owner's manual." Then we complain because we don't know how things work. The problems are not with the manufacturer or the equipment. The problems are with our own ignorance. I learned one thing from my experiences. I need to read my owner's manual, the Bible.

Our Honeymoon cruise took us to Nassau, San Juan and St. Thomas in the Caribbean. It was a little chilly at times, but we had a great time. We met a couple from Tucson, AZ. He was the director of the Tucson Boys Chorus. We did some things with them on shore excursions and enjoyed their company at the shows on board ship in the evenings.

One of the things we did was go scuba diving in St. Thomas. It turned out to be an experience that reminded me of my skiing trip with Sherryl. None of us had ever done any scuba diving before. We all thought it would be fun to try. We signed up for a shore excursion that included novice training and a short dive.

Sherryl and our friends seemed to have no trouble at all with the entire experience. I, on the other hand, had problems right from the start. We were fitted for equipment and headed to the water for further instructions. I couldn't believe how heavy the tank and weight belts were. I figured they would make me sink like a rock. Wrong! Once in the water I seemed to have more trouble than anyone else staying under the surface. I couldn't believe how hard it was just to keep from floating to the top. Besides that, water continually leaked into my mask. I think it was because of my mustache. Everybody else seemed to be swimming along fine. I couldn't keep my rear end from wanting to lead me straight to the surface and I was constantly blind because of the water in my mask. For one instant I was close to panic! I considered giving up the rest of the dive and going in. Then I thought about having to hear how I chickened out from Sherryl for the rest of my life. I decided it would be better to drown! I continue through the whole dive. My mask always at least half full of water. I joke about it now and tell people I had a little fish swimming in it. I really didn't, but I was glad when the whole thing was over.

On Wednesday night the cruise ship had a talent night. Passengers that wanted to be in the show went earlier in the day to audition. Our friends from Tucson were going to do "Country Roads" as a duet. I knew Sherryl would like to sing, so I told her I would audition too. Sherryl sang "Evergreen" a Barbara Striesan song. I sang "Chantilly Lace" by the Big Bopper. Boy how my life had changed! Just a few days earlier I sang in public for the first time at my own wedding. Now I was singing in front of eight hundred people on a cruise ship. The genie was out of the bottle!

Sherryl and I both loved the whole cruise experience. We had a great honeymoon. If you have never been on a cruise, we highly recommend it. What is so nice is never having to decide where to eat or worrying about prices. There is built in entertainment every night as well. We were both surprised by how small our room was, but you are not in it very much and they clean your room every time you leave for more than five minutes.

The food was great. Once at dinner, Sherryl ordered a seafood entree and our waiter suggested she get something else. Sherryl wanted to stick with her choice so the waiter asked her what her second choice would be. When he returned with our meals he brought Sher both of her selections. She didn't like the seafood dish at all. Our waiter told her, "See, next time maybe you will listen to your waiter." They really took good care of us. If we could afford it, Sherryl and I would take a cruise every year.

When we returned home the changes in our lives continued to come one right after another. The first day Sherryl went back to work she came home and said, "Do you want to be in the hospital follies?" I had no idea what the hospital follies even were, let alone knowing if I wanted to be in them, but it was easy to see that Sher wanted to do it, so I did too. We headed right back up to her hospital that night and landed parts in the follies.

The follies are a fund raising show the hospital puts on every other year. Sherryl had been in them before and this time she wanted me to share the experience with her. It was a lot of fun. I was surprised by the size of the whole production. We did two shows that sold out a two thousand seat theater in Lorain, Oh. We were in several parts of the show as well as the large chorus that sang at the end. It took up a lot of evenings rehearsing for a couple of weeks, but we both really enjoyed it.

Other changes kept coming. My sister Glenda was

encouraging me to sing a solo at church. It was a pretty lively song for our little country church. She was also working on creating a gospel quartet with Sherryl and I joining Chuck and Linda. Chuck was a distant cousin of Sherryl's and he and Linda attended Penfield Church too.

Chuck and Linda had both been married before, just like we had. Chuck had received a "Dear John" letter while he was in Vietnam. Linda also had a husband who was unfaithful to her. Chuck was the bass, Linda the soprano, Sherryl the alto and I was the tenor. Now I wasn't only singing, I was learning to sing harmony! If you had known me before you would add this to the list of miracles we had.

When I was in high school I tried out for the choir. I was one of a handful that weren't allowed to join. When I had my rock band I was always asking to sing. They never let me. How things were changing. Suddenly people were asking me to sing. It still amazes me.

The first song the quartet learned was "Must Jesus Bear The Cross Alone." It was easy for Sherryl and Chuck. They read music and were great at singing harmony. Linda had been an excellent singer for years as well, although she didn't read music and usually sang melody. I took a while to learn my harmony part, but with Glenda's help and encouragement, it began to come together. We started to practice regularly. Linda thought up our group's name, "Second Chance."

The start up of "Second Chance Ministries" brought us much closer to Chuck and Linda than we had been before. Both of them had done work in plays that were put on by a theater group in Wellington. They were going to try out for parts in a local production of "Harvey." The movie "Harvey" starred Jimmy Stewart as a man who was friends with a six foot tall invisible rabbit. Chuck and Linda encouraged Sherryl and me to audition. Chuck landed the leading role of Mr. Dowd. Linda was the psychiatrist's wife. Sherryl was the nurse at the asylum and I was Mr. Wilson the strong arm orderly. It was another first for both Sherryl and me. We had a great time doing it.

Our contemporary gospel quartet was the thing that really caught our interest. I was looking for chances to give my testimony. We were learning more and more music all the time. It wasn't long before we started going to sing at other churches and various functions.

Glenda, Sherryl, our Pastor's daughter Linda Rugg and I also started holding meetings to inform people about issues that Christians needed to be aware of. We called them "CATCH" meetings (Citizens Alerted To Critical Happenings). We talked about abortion, education, pornography and evolution. Most of all we tried to educate people about "Secular Humanism" and help them see how it was involved in all these areas. I wrote a lot of editorials as well. We succeeded in stirring up the pot a little. I am sure that more than a few people in Wellington probably used the phrase, "Gordy got religion" when talking about me. I didn't get religion. I got Jesus! I learned the truth. I had met the Truth! I wanted others to meet Him.

With all these changes going on in our lives we were excited. We wanted people to know that God really exists and He knows us. Around May of 1983 I wrote to the "700 Club"(Pat Robertson's T.V. program) and told them about my experience. That summer they sent a crew to Wellington and taped a segment for the program. It aired later that year.

My life had changed so much so quickly. I was happy. I was very happy.

# Chapter Thirteen

# The Attack

ometimes things can be going so well, that you have
to pinch yourself to be sure you're not dreaming. That
is how our lives had been since our midnight wedding
January 1st of 1982.

Sherryl and I were living an adventure. We had done
things we had never done before. We were ministering for
the Lord in the gospel quartet. We were in the follies. We
were in the play "Harvey." We even made movies. I'm not
kidding. All four members of "Second Chance" also acted in
a few Christian films.

The films were definitely low budget. No budget would be
a better description. They were produced and directed by John
Martin. John was a young Christian man from Elyria, Ohio.
Even though the films were low budget they contained a solid
Christian message. They provided John with the opportunity
to give his testimony in several churches throughout the area
and they provided all of us with great memories.

We were enjoying our families like we never had before.

We bowled in a couples league every other Sunday evening with my parents as our partners. After bowling we would play cards with them, and my sister and brother-in-law and my niece and nephew. Sherryl bowled in a women's league on Thursdays. Her team was made up of my mom, her mom, her former mother-in-law, and her sisters. I bowled on Wednesdays with my dad and Glenda's husband Roger. In the summers, Sherryl played slow pitch soft ball with her sisters and friends. I played fast pitch soft ball with her brother Rick. I played golf with her brothers Rick and Ron whenever we could. I think you get the picture. We were simply having a great time.

Our little country church was growing in spirit and in numbers. The (CATCH) meetings we put on, the editorials we wrote, and the things we said whenever we sang, were done because we felt led to do them. The Penfield United Church Of Christ was having theological differences with things the denomination headquarters were saying and doing. Eventually the church voted overwhelmingly to leave the denomination. It became the Penfield Community Church.

Our Christian lives and our personal lives were fulfilling, fun, and interesting. For me, I was enjoying a married life that I couldn't even conceive of before. In the midst of all this, I suddenly received a warning from the Lord.

I was driving home after church. Sherryl wasn't with me. We had driven separate vehicles that morning. I can't remember why. Driving separately wasn't uncommon for us. We were involved in so many things, that we often took two cars.

As I headed home, I had another spiritual experience. I didn't hear a voice like I had when Jesus kept me from driving into the tree. This was different. It wasn't audible like my previous experience. It was more like a thought being placed in my mind. It didn't come from me. It just suddenly was there. "Someone in Second Chance was going to be attacked."

That was the message, the warning. I was suddenly very frightened. The message was clear, but that was all it contained. "Someone in Second Chance was going to be attacked." I had no idea which one of us would be the target. I had no idea what form the attack was going to take. I just knew it was coming.

I was so sure that an attack was coming and that the warning was genuine that I felt compelled to drive straight over to Chuck and Linda's house. They were already home from church. I rang the bell. When they came to the door I told them we needed to talk.

Chuck and Linda had a nice screened in back porch. That's where we went. I told them the message I had just received. I let them know that I was convinced it was a warning from the Lord. I wanted them to know that I was taking it very seriously. I told them they needed to think about whether they should continue in "Second Chance." If they remained in the group, the attack could be against one of them. They knew I was serious. They could tell that whatever it was I just experienced, it really shook me up. They were going to keep singing. "Second Chance" would continue.

I told Sherryl what happened. I let her know that I took the warning very seriously. I was sure it was from the Lord. An attack was coming. One of "Second Chance" was the target.

The warning had been plain and it scared me. Three weeks had passed since it had been delivered. Nothing had changed. Just about the time I was beginning to forget about it, the changes started.

Sherryl began to have some headaches. She had an eye exam and they found that she needed glasses. She started wearing glasses and for a few days she seemed to be better. Right at this time, Sherryl's dad needed a bucket truck driven from Ohio out to her brother Ron in California. We could arrange our work schedules to be able to do this for him and we thought it would be fun. We would be able to visit Ron and his family for a couple of days and then fly home. We would even earn a little extra money at the same time.

Driving the bucket truck to California wasn't as much fun as we expected. The truck was much slower than driving a car. It was much less comfortable. Worst of all, Sherryl started suffering from more severe headaches. We completed the task and as soon as we got back home, Sherryl went to see her doctor.

The initial diagnosis was that Sherryl was suffering from migraine headaches. She was given a prescription to use for pain and we went home. During the next three weeks the headaches intensified. Finally one day they became so severe that she vomited. Nothing seemed to alleviate her pain. I took her to the hospital where she worked. Her doctor ordered a CAT scan.

Sherryl knew everyone that worked in x-ray. When the scan was over, she asked the technicians if they found anything. They told her that they weren't allowed to read the scan. The doctors would read it and let her know. Sherryl knew already. The scan had found something. She could read it in their faces.

I was out front in the waiting area, praying and hoping that everything would be fine. I know I wasn't alone, but I can't remember who was there with me. It probably was my parents and Sherryl's mom. When Sherryl's doctor came out, the news was like getting punched in the heart. Sherryl had a brain tumor.

It was Thursday May 31$^{st}$, 1984. They kept Sherryl in the hospital that evening to do more scans and some other tests. We had a lot of decisions to make. She was going to have brain surgery. We needed to decide who was going to do it and where it was going to be done. The first inclination when you live in northern Ohio is to go to the Cleveland Clinic. Sherryl wanted to have it done where she worked, Lorain Community Hospital. She knew the people at

Community Hospital and she knew they would do all they could for her. She was given a very good recommendation for a neural surgeon at Community. She decided to have him do the surgery. His name was Dr. Sertich.

That Thursday had been a long and trying day. Sherryl handled the news almost with a sigh of relief. She was frightened, but at least now she knew what the problem was. She would hear the recommendations on how to handle the tumor, make the best decisions, and trust in the Lord.

Dr. Sertich wanted Sherryl to have testing done to measure her field of peripheral vision. He was concerned that the area the tumor was in could cause her some permanent peripheral vision loss. Sherryl had to see Dr. Costin, an optometrist. Sherryl had tried to see Dr. Costin when she had her eyes examined, but he was so busy that she couldn't get in to see him for several months. When he learned that Sherryl had a brain tumor, he felt terrible that he hadn't been able to see her. After he examined her, he asked Sherryl if she would mind if he prayed with her. Of course Sherryl didn't mind at all. She was so impressed by the wonderful prayer he said for her. Dr. Costin prayed for everyone involved with the surgery. He prayed that every doctor and nurse would do their job flawlessly. Sherryl never forgot that wonderful prayer. She understood why Dr. Costin was always so busy. He is a very special doctor.

That evening after all the decisions had been made and everyone else had gone home, we remember being together at her hospital bed. We were both feeling pretty sorry for ourselves. We were shedding tears together. It was strange, but right at the same time, we both had the same thought. We looked around us at the other patients on the floor. We realized that as bad as we felt our circumstances were, there were people all around us, some with more dire conditions than we faced. Sherryl calmed me down. We prayed, and after she fell asleep, I went home.

The next morning was a Friday. Before I got to the hospital they had the schedule set. Sherryl would be operated on at 8:00 am Monday June 4th. They were going to release her today so that she could be home with Chad and I over the weekend. I was to bring her back to the Hospital Sunday afternoon. Sherryl called me at home to let me know that I didn't have to come and pick her up. At that time the hospital operated a Trauma Unit that had a life flight helicopter. The Trauma Team decided that they were going to give Sherryl a ride home in the chopper. We lived in the country about twenty five miles south of the hospital. We had a large yard where they could land easily. They wanted to show Sherryl how they did their job. Like an angel she returned home from the sky in a special taxi driven by her friends.

Because "Second Chance" had been to many area churches, word spread quickly about Sherryl's upcoming surgery. We had also been involved in helping an independent candidate campaign for Congress. He was a solid Christian man. When he heard about Sherryl, he came to our church service that Sunday, June 3rd. He designed a prayer chart that had people commit to 15 minute blocks of time. People signed up and pledged to pray for Sherryl. Between His home church, our church at Penfield and The Assembly of God Church in Wellington where Sherryl's sister Debbie and her husband Ben attended, Sherryl had someone praying for her around the clock for the next 72 hours. It was truly a humbling experience for both of us to see how people responded to help Sherryl.

One of our dear friends in Christ, Gerry Hall gave Sherryl a get well card. In it Gerry told how Christ had given her the Scripture John 11:4, to give to Sherryl. "This sickness will not end in death. No, it is for God's glory so that God's Son may be glorified through it." the verse says. Now this is a scripture that many people who are sick turn to for comfort, but Gerry said the Lord gave it to her and Sherryl claimed it.

It meant a great deal to her and she clung to it.

That morning in church we anointed Sherryl with oil and everyone gathered around her. With us all touching one another and with as many as could laying hands on Sherryl, we prayed. Sherryl and I don't know how people can make it through the tough times in life without the Lord and a church family. We can't understand why anyone would want to try.

We have so many friends that are our brothers and sisters in Christ. "People Need The Lord," is the title of one of our favorite songs. People also need each other. We love so many people through our common bonds with the Church and the Lord. The value of these relationships comes at a cost, however. This large extended family means that we share their sorrows and pain. We help each other in times of need. We grieve with one another in times of loss. We also rejoice with each other in times of victory or success. When a church is what God intends for it to be, it plays an essential role in people's lives.

I took Sherryl back to the hospital early Sunday evening and stayed with her through the night. Early Monday morning they began the task of preparing her for surgery. I went out to the waiting area and sat with a large number of family and friends. Each of us had little to say as we continually cast up silent prayers for Sherryl.

The surgery took almost nine hours. It was the longest nine hours of my life. I was OK for the first three hours and then it really began to weigh on me. We were given some updates as to how things were going and they told us it would be quite a while until the surgeon was finished. Eventually, I had to get away from everyone else and find a place to be alone. I had heard all the small talk and speculation that people always have when waiting through this type of thing. I needed space.

I got up and went outside. I walked across a large expanse

of parking lot to a grassy area north of the hospital. I found a spot where I didn't think anyone would notice me and I laid down. With my face to the ground I started to talk with God. I reminded Him of what He told me. "You said that it was as bad as it was going to get for me. You kept me from driving into that tree. You gave me Sherryl. You have made my life happier and more complete than I ever imagined. If you take Sherryl, it will be worse for me than it was! Please, you have to realize that! I need her. Chad needs her. Please don't take her from us." I prayed like that, reminding God over and over again about his promise to me. Finally after about two hours out there on the grass, I sensed a reply. I didn't hear it like before and it wasn't as sure as the warning message had been but it seemed to be there. "You're right, I promised and I haven't forgotten. Trust Me. You do trust Me, don't you?"

I felt a peace. He wouldn't lie to me. I know how much He loves me. I had felt that unbelievable degree of love. Trust Him. What else could I do?

Finally the surgery was over. We met with Dr. Sertich and he told us what he had found. Sherryl had a golf ball size tumor that was well encapsulated he explained. It had been easy for him to distinguish between healthy tissue and diseased tissue. By the looks of the tumor he felt it was most likely a grade two Astrocytoma. A malignant tumor that Sherryl and I had read about over the weekend. The average life expectancy for patients with this type of tumor was about seven to eight years. Dr. Surdich went on to say that the tumor had some strange looking cells and he couldn't be sure what it was until the pathology report was in. We would get that report in a few days. Sherryl had come through the surgery fine.

The news was not everything we wanted to hear, but it could have been much worse. Sherryl and I had gone to her medical textbooks and read up on brain tumors. We had hoped the tumor would not be cancerous, but we had learned that many benign tumors can be just as deadly as malignant ones. The news was not great, but it could have been worse. For the moment it was a welcomed relief to know that I had at least a few more years to look forward to with my bride.

The actual physical part of the surgery had gone better than anyone had prepared us for. We were told that Sherryl would have all her head shaved. It turned out that she only had about a five inch circle shaved behind her right ear. Her son Chad was eight years old. Chad had all of his hair cut off to surprise his Mom and show sympathy for her plight. It turned out Sherryl had a lot more hair than Chad did. They told us Sherryl would probably have black and blue areas around her eyes and a lot of swelling. That never showed up. Except for a very sore left side because she laid on it in the same position for nine hours, she felt fine. The only outward signs anything had happened was the circle of missing hair and the bandage that covered it.

Friday evening June 8th, they released Sherryl from the hospital. The next day was Saturday and a party had been planned for my parents 50th anniversary. Their anniversary was actually June 12th, but the weekend party had been planned for several months. Everyone was surprised when Sherryl showed up for the party. She not only showed up, "Second Chance" sang three songs.

Everything was going better than anyone expected. The next morning was Sunday. Those who attended church Sunday, that hadn't been at my parents party, were amazed to see Sherryl there. She was not only there, she looked great. She wore this little red head scarf that hid any signs of her surgery. People couldn't believe how great she was doing. Everyone was reveling in the answer to prayer they were seeing right before their eyes. We gave everyone an update on all the information we had. Everyone pledged to continue to pray that the pathology report would come back benign.

Sherryl was to go back to Dr. Sertich's office to have her staples removed on Monday. That was all that we expected for this visit. It was only going to take a few minutes. Since I had been missing work we made plans to have Sherryl's friend Jeanene drive her to the appointment. God had other plans.

# Chapter Fourteen

# *Time of Special Trial*

※

Jeanene and Sherryl had been friends since high school. Jeanene and her husband Bob went to Penfield Church, like we did. The four of us had been friends from the time Sherryl and I began dating. Dr. Sertich hadn't cleared Sherryl to drive yet, so someone had to take her wherever she needed to go. Since Sherryl was only going to have her staples removed from the surgery, Jeanene volunteered to take her to the appointment. Afterwards the two of them were going to do some shopping. This allowed me to go to work.

So many strange and unplanned things happened that day. None of us can recall all of them. We all know now that the hand of God was involved in every one of them. Something happened with my work. I can't recall exactly what, but it required me to return home early that afternoon. Jeanene's car broke down in the parking lot of the shopping center that was located about a quarter mile in front of Dr. Sertich's office. The clutch had gone out of Jeanene's car. Sherryl and Jeanene went into the department store, and when no other source of help could be found, out of desperation, Sherryl called home. She didn't expect me to be there, but she figured she could leave me a message. I was home and they were relieved when I told them I would come up right away. It would take me about 40-minutes to get to them, but it was a while until Sherryl's appointment. She would get to Dr. Sertich on time and we would get Jeanene's car somewhere for repairs.

As I went to pull out of my driveway the mailman's car was just delivering our mail. I stopped, grabbed the mail and set it on the front seat beside me. It was a hot, sun shining, clear blue day in June. I didn't have any trouble finding Jeanene's car. When I got there, the girls were waiting by it. I can't remember if we had time to get her car to a repair shop before the appointment or if we just got a wrecker to tow it. However things happened, we did get Sherryl to Dr. Sertich's office. I went in and stayed in the waiting room while Dr. Sertich removed Sherryl's staples. It didn't take very long at all. When the procedure was finished, Dr. Sertich summoned me into the room. He had received the pathology report. His face betrayed the news.

"It's a grade 4 glioblastoma." Dr. Sertich said. Sherryl and I both knew what that meant. We read about all the types of brain tumors in her textbooks. Cancerous brain tumors are rated on a scale of 1 to 4. A grade 4 glioblastoma was the worst type. Her textbooks gave a median life expectancy of six months, a maximum life expectancy of one to two years. Dr. Sertich went on to tell us that the tumor he removed seemed well encapsulated, but that it did have strange looking cells. Even though he was able to remove all of the tumor he found, a grade 4 glioblastoma probably had microscopic strands of cancerous cells that were too small to be seen. He said he expected the tumor to reappear within three to six months.

It was like being run over by a truck. Everything had been

going so well. The miracle everyone was praying for had seemed to happen. We expected that the pathology report would bring surprisingly good news. Our hopes had been so high and our faith so strong. We expected to hear that the tumor was benign, and it was totally removed. Just go on with your life, the problem is solved. That is what we expected to hear. Instead, we got the worst possible report from pathology.

While Sherryl and I stood there in stunned silence, Dr. Sertich explained that Sherryl faced a high probability of future surgeries. He said the next step he would recommend would be to go through radiation therapy. He didn't think chemotherapy should be done. Sherryl and I both asked him more questions. I can't remember everything we discussed. I do remember the final things he said to us. He told us the Cleveland Clinic was doing a research study on an experimental neutron radiation. The treatments could only be done at the NASA Lewis Research Center by Cleveland Airport. Because of Sherryl's age and her young son Chad, he had recommended her for the program. We were to come back in a week to learn just how the radiation treatments would be scheduled.

Jeanene was waiting for us in the back seat of my car. She wondered what had taken us so long. She could see that something was terribly wrong. When we got into the car and told Jeanene about the pathology report and the radiation that was to come, we all started crying together. Sherryl was handling it better than we were, but it was easy to see that she was scared. She would cry the hardest when she thought about Chad and me. She didn't want to let us down. She worried about what would become of her two boys. Sherryl wasn't about to accept a death sentence. "Gerry gave me John 11:4 and I'm still going to claim it." She sobbed.

Our pain and sorrow steadily grew. The ability for any of us to hold back the tears was long gone when Sherryl saw the mail on the front seat between us. On the top of the pile was an envelope with a return address of Freeman, South Dakota. "Who do we know in South Dakota?" Sherryl asked.

"I don't know," I answered her as she opened it.

At that point in our lives, we needed God. We needed to know that He was still there. That He hadn't forsaken us. Looking back on the events of that day, He had been watching out for us all along. He knew that Sherryl shouldn't receive that pathology report all by her self. He had arranged things so that I would be there with her. Not only that, He arranged things so that we had exactly what we needed, exactly when we needed it.

I can't write this even now without tears welling up. Inside the envelope was a simple little get well card. On the front was a picture of a little girl sitting on a split rail fence with her hand reaching out feeding a little squirrel. Above the picture it said, "Please Hurry and Get Well." On the inside, at the bottom of the page it read, "Cast your burden upon the Lord and He will sustain you…" Psalms 55:22. On the inside of the back page it had written across the top, "Freeman, S. Dak. June 9th 1984. Dear Cheryl, (spelled wrong, everyone spells Sherryl's name wrong) "Get well quickly, Please, please do, We want to see you back again, because we all miss you." Those were the words on the card from the manufacturer. Then it read, "Yes, I miss you, even so far away, and my prayers are with you. I know God is going to bring glory to Himself out of your illness, *John 11:4*. "This sickness will not end in death. No, it is for God's glory so that God's Son may be glorified through it." May He strengthen, comfort, encourage and sustain you and your family as you trust Him during this time of special trial. The three sisters are having a super time together. How good God is to give us these joys along the way. Be of good cheer! Love in Christ, Ruth Hege."

This card not only said what we needed to hear, it was a

confirmation of the scripture Gerry Hall had received for Sherryl. Confirmation right when we needed it the most. But the most amazing thing about it, was who sent it to us. Ruth Hege was truly one of God's special saints. This little elderly women had served the Lord all her life. She had been a missionary in the Belgium Congo and seen her fellow servants of God murdered by the natives. She wrote a book about that experience entitled "We Two Alone." Ruth Hege knew Jesus! More than anyone we had ever known, Ruth had the Lord oozing out of her. She was a special lady and she had been attending our little church in Penfield for the past year. She was out in South Dakota with one of her sisters to visit the third sibling. She had written Sherryl this card as soon as she learned about the brain surgery she faced. God saw to it that we received this message exactly at the time we had to have it. It was a miracle! It was a confirmation!

The message on the card form Ruth Hege calmed all three of us. "Nobody knows how long he is going to live." Sherryl said. "We could get hit by a car tomorrow." Sherryl would handle this problem the same way she handled everything. She would do what she could and then she would trust God. We would do what the doctors recommended and leave the rest up to the Lord. It would be a lie to suggest that we both weren't still scared by it all, but God had given us enough help and friends to see us through.

Sherryl was accepted into the experimental radiation study that the Cleveland Clinic was doing. This meant that she had regular cobalt radiation alternated with the experimental neutron radiation at the NASA Lewis Research Center. Radiation therapy does not cause all the side effects that chemotherapy can (at least not at the time it is done). Sherryl never got sick or felt bad. The only physical effects were getting tired from the trips to get the radiation done, and the loss of her beautiful blonde hair. The treatments lasted about six weeks. They were done every other day.

Once they were finished, Sherryl had to have a CAT scan done every other month at first. When no sign of the tumor ever showed up in the scans, time between scans was lengthen to 6 months and then to once a year.

A year after Sherryl's tumor was removed a feature story about her appeared in the Lorain Journal Newspaper. Written by Don Shilling, I thought it would be good to include it here. In a feature section that was called "Turning Points" here is what the article said.

"One day in June last year, Sherryl Perkins came home from her doctor's office and dug out an old nursing textbook.

She looked for the section on brain tumors. Then the part on grade four tumors, the worst malignant brain tumors possible.

She found what her doctor would not tell her: "life expectancy, six months to two years."

Now nearly a year later, at age thirty two, Mrs. Perkins believes she has found out something else which her doctor will not tell her.

"No doctor will say I'm healed. But I say I'm healed. What is faith but evidence of things unseen? And I've got that faith," she said.

Mrs. Perkins had neurosurgery last June. Just three months later she was back to work as a nurse at Lorain Community Hospital.

Now She is trying, and succeeding, to return her life to what it was.

Because she suffers no brain damage from the tumor, it has been relatively easy physically. Preparing herself mentally, of course, has been harder.

Mrs. Perkins, a nurse at the hospital for the past 11 years, had been dealt the worst blow life has to offer—she had been told she was soon to die. But rather than destroy her, the bad news focused her on the important things of her life.

Rather than worry about her cancer, she concentrates on

God, her family, her friends and the natural beauty which surrounds her.

"I've got a 35-minute drive home from work, and all I do is reflect. I think about my gratitude, my thankfulness. I'm really thankful for all my friends and all the cards I've received," she said.

In addition, she has hope. And with good reason.

Her doctor said that even with her radiation treatments, he expected the cancer to return by last November. Her latest tests, done this month, show no return of the tumor which was operated on last June.

Mrs. Perkins is back working at the hospital 24 hours a week as a staff development assistant. She is a registered nurse and chose to work part time just before her tumor was diagnosed.

She lives on Stewart Rd. just south of Wellington with her husband Gordon. She has a son, Chad 8 and two stepchildren, Tracy 15 and Kyley Perkins, 11.

All of Mrs. Perkins' hope isn't based on her bold claim of being healed. She simply wants to live.

"I live my life as if I'm going to live forever. But it doesn't matter to me that I've had a brain tumor. Anyone can be struck by a car and die at any time. I'm not at any more risk than anyone else," she said.

But she also faces up to her cancer. In fact, she is prepared to die.

"Obviously, when I found out it was a grade four tumor I thought about dying. But I wasn't afraid for myself. I just didn't want to leave my son, and I didn't want to leave my husband," she said.

"But as for me, I am not afraid of where I am going," she added.

Mrs. Perkins' faith in God has seen her through. It was shaken when doctors discovered after an eight-hour surgery that the tumor was a grade four tumor rather than a less serious grade two as was expected.

"I was devastated. For two or three days I cried with my husband. But then I got it out of my system," she said.

For her husband, Gordon, 36, the struggle to maintain confidence in God despite the tumor was tougher.

"My husband is a little less sure," she said. "But I think the person who is affected always has more faith than the person who may be left behind."

Gordon was especially shaken by the news, she said, because they both had been married before, but, "This time we knew we had found the right thing," she said.

Even before recent months when she began to think she may be cured, she concentrated on life, not death. Mrs. Perkins said she went through her radiation treatments, and she lost her hair, but she never felt like there "was impending doom."

Also, she never worried about the two-year limit the textbook placed on her life. In fact, she said, she never experienced anger over her cancer. She had never even thought about being angry until a nurse in the intensive care unit told her she should be angry.

"Why should I be angry?" she remembers telling the nurse. "It would be a waste of effort, a waste of my emotions. I've got it, and I must accept it."

In fact, just six days after her surgery she was singing with her gospel group, Second Chance, at her husband's parents 50th wedding anniversary.

Of course, the little things can be the hardest.

"I cried for a week when I lost my hair. In fact, I cried more over losing my hair than when I found out I had cancer," she said.

She was slicking her hair back one Saturday after she had been swimming. Clumps of hair began coming out and by Sunday night, her hair was all gone.

Conversely, little things are often the nicest.

Before going into surgery, she had told her son Chad, then 7 that she would have her head clean-shaven. Only part of the right side of her head actually needed to be shaved, however. But Chad was never told.

When he came in to see his mother after surgery, his hair was clipped into a short crew cut.

"I said 'No, Chad, I love your hair.' But he did it for his mom so she wouldn't feel bad," Mrs. Perkins said.

Now her son's hair is back. Her hair is mostly back, too. On the surface it appears as if nothing has changed except her having to undergo periodic tests.

But, in reality, her cancer has given her a whole new meaning and a whole new outlook on life.

She is thankful for the love of her family, thankful for her church members' prayers, thankful that she can still work and thankful that she can still sing. In other words, thankful for life."

\* \* \*

It was a very nice story and I think it gives you a sense of what Sherryl is like. The end of the story, where it says Sherryl was given a whole new outlook on life, isn't very accurate. Sherryl always had a great outlook on life. The way she dealt with the cancer was amazing, but it is how she deals with everything.

One thing Sherryl says she learned, is to be careful what you pray for, because you may get it. She said that during the first two years of our marriage, she envied how on fire I was for the Lord. Sherryl said that she prayed that the Lord would do something to shake her up. Well, she was shaken up all right. The trouble was it shook me up, and everyone else who loved her up, too!

Second Chance Ministries' name, now had a second meaning. Originally it was chosen because of the second marriages that God had given us. Now the healing that Sherryl received, added new meaning to our name.

Sherryl gave her testimony wherever we were invited to sing. Gerry Hall and Ruth Hege had received a word from the Lord that John 11:4 was going to be fulfilled in Sherryl's trial. Sherryl did exactly that for the next several years. "This sickness will not end in death. No, it is for God's glory, so that God's Son may be glorified through it."

When Sherryl passed the two year mark after surgery with no sign of the tumor recurring, Dr. Sertich told her to forget about it. It wasn't coming back. The Cleveland Clinic called four different pathologist's to review the slides from her tumor. The experimental neutron radiation program she went through was deemed unsuccessful. All the other patients died, as expected. None showed any benefits from it. Since the radiation couldn't be credited with Sherryl's still being alive, the doctors needed to find an explanation. Four referee pathologists reviewed her case. Three of them confirmed that Sherryl had a grade 4 glioblastoma. One pathologist said that Sherryl had something else, a pleomorphic xantho astrocytoma.

This one varying opinion bothered Sherryl. She felt as though this doctor was trying to steal her miracle. That is exactly what Sherryl would tell people when she gave her testimony. Three out of four doctors had no other explanation except a miracle. Even if the fourth was right and it was a different type of tumor, than God had answered our prayers in that way. God definitely was glorified just like He said He would be.

# Chapter Fifteen

# *Life Goes On*

Except for the loss of Sherryl's long beautiful blonde hair and the need for an MRI every two years, there wasn't much change in our lives. The next eight years following the removal of the brain tumor "Second Chance Ministries" continued to sing and spread the good news. Our little church at Penfield continued to grow. Sherryl and I remained active just like before, with the exception of her softball pitching.

Our lives were pretty much back to normal, for us. I was enjoying doing some sports play by play for our local high school teams. Glenda's husband Roger was very interested in the cable TV local access station for Wellington. Roger had been mayor of Wellington when cable TV was first made available to the community. He ran the access channel for several years. It was another enjoyable opportunity for me. It was also training for plans God had in store for Penfield Community Church.

Life had its ups and downs. Most of the time we had ups,

but we weren't immune from having our share of downs as well.

On the up side, Sherryl became the Lorain County Nurse of Hope for the American Cancer Society. This allowed her to touch even more people with her testimony. I won an Eagle Award with my employer Betz Laboratories. That allowed me to give my testimony and tell about Sherryl's miracle to all of our division's salesmen at the awards banquet in Houston, TX. "Second Chance Ministries" averaged about fifteen to twenty appearances per year for the next ten years. In addition to those things, Sherryl and I just got closer and closer to each others parents and families. Life was very good.

Sherryl and I went on our second seven day cruise in the Caribbean in May of 1988. We went with Dave and Teresa. Dave was Sherryl's age and had been a fan of my rock band "The Bent Twigs" way back in 1966. Dave was finishing the eighth grade then and he was the Bent Twigs first and only groupie. He and Sherryl were class mates at Wellington and had dated a couple of times during high school. Dave and Teresa starting attending Penfield Community Church about the same time Sherryl and I did. Dave learned how to play guitar during high school and played lead guitar in different groups for several years. When Second Chance started up, Dave was God's gift to us. He began running our sound almost from day one. Teresa graduated from nearby Keystone High School the same year as Dave and Sherryl. We had known each other for years and were great friends.

Sherryl and I finally talked Dave and Teresa into going on a cruise with us. It didn't start out so well. We didn't have a lot of money so we both had one of the lowest priced cabins. We tried to prepare them for how small the rooms were, but they were still shocked when they first saw them. What made it even worse was that Dave and Teresa's room had a musty odor to it. We were on a lower deck in the stern of the ship. Dave later would jokingly tell people that he and Teresa had to grease the ship's propeller shaft every night before they went to bed, because it traveled though their room. Fortunately the odor went away and Dave and Teresa quickly adapted to the room size.

I had mistakenly told Dave that once on board they didn't have to pay for anything to eat or drink unless they got an alcoholic beverage. That wasn't totally true. We found at our first dinner seating that we had to pay for carbonated beverages also. Now, Dave isn't the biggest spender in the world. When the wine girl told him he had to pay for carbonated drinks, Dave didn't take it too well. We laugh about it now, but Dave really gave that poor girl a tough time. It was her first cruise and we were one of the first tables she ever served. Dave's reaction to her just about ended her career right then. By about mid cruise Dave had made up with her and she could approach our table without that fearful look in her eyes.

We ended up having a great time. We had some adventures with Sherryl on the shore excursions that made her the celebrity of our tour bus in St. Croix. Dave and Teresa were sitting across from us in the back of the bus. The tour bus was just a converted old school bus. Sherryl had the window seat and I was next to her in the isle seat. The driver pulled off the road and told everyone that the big house located on top of the hill in front of us belonged to actress Maureen O'Hara. The driver expected to get right back underway, but Sherryl ask him to wait and told me to go out and take some video and a picture of the house. I said, "No, we don't need video of a house." Sherryl insisted that we did and gave me a nudge. Actually she pushed me right off the seat and I landed on the floor in the isle of the bus. I surrendered and reluctantly made the embarrassing walk up the isle with the video camera. I went outside and took the pictures.

Everywhere the tour bus took us, Sherryl was the last one

to get back on board. It happened at the rum factory we visited, in the town we stopped to shop at, and last of all at the botanical gardens we visited. By this time everyone knew Sherryl and me.

The tour stayed at the gardens for about an hour. When it got time to get back on the bus, Sherryl had to go to the bathroom. Everyone else was on the bus and waiting to leave except Sherryl. Suddenly the bus started to pull out. I jumped up out of my seat and yelled, "Wait a minute, my wife isn't here yet!" Then I paused and said, "On second thought, go ahead."

Everyone laughed and the bus driver got into the spirit of things. He went ahead and pulled the bus out of the parking space it had been in and onto the road. When Sherryl came out of the restroom she walked over to the parking lot. Everyone on the bus was watching now, to see how she would react. When she saw the bus was gone she started looking all around in a panic. Finally, she spotted the bus sitting on the road about fifty yards away. She started to run to catch it. As she got close, the driver started slowly pulling forward. It may sound a little cruel, but really it was great fun. When the driver finally stopped and let her get on board, we had everyone ask her at the same time, "Did everything come out all right?."

Our waiter on this cruise was a handsome young Italian. He was about twenty-one years old. His name was Gianni. He was very nice and we had a lot of fun with him all during the week. Sherryl and Teresa always let us know how good looking he was. To this day, whenever we mention the name Gianni to Sherryl, the next three words out of her mouth are, "He's so cute!" If I wasn't so secure in our love, Gianni would have made me jealous.

This cruise had a talent night just like our honeymoon cruise did. I did some stand up comedy, mostly telling stories about Sherryl and our cruise experiences. I even mentioned our waiter Gianni. His name brought a nice applause. I told everyone how I thought his last name must be, "He's so cute," because Sherryl said those words every time she heard his name. It went pretty well. The folks who had been on the tour bus with us really enjoyed the stories. In some ways Sherryl has always reminded me of Lucy on the "I love Lucy" show. You never know what will happen. You just know it will be interesting.

Dave and I even went scuba diving again at the same place Sherryl and I went on our honeymoon. This time I didn't have any trouble. We all had a great time. Someday I hope we can go again with even more friends.

I don't know how Sherryl did it, but when we came back home from the airport, there was a surprise 40th birthday party waiting for me. Boy, was I surprised! That is Sherryl though, she is always surprising me.

On the down side, there where some personal trials and tragedies.

Sherryl's father had started a company called "Energized Substation Service." He had worked with electricity with the local rural electric co-op. He left that job to work with a man who had this insulator cleaning business. The man retired and "Chip," Sherryl's dad bought the business. Sherryl's mom "Donna" wasn't please with the move and the insecurity of being in business for themselves, but it turned out to be a very smart business move. The combination of Chip's work ethic and Donna's money management made them very successful.

The company he started provided a substantial income and a place for Sherryl's brothers Rick and Ron to work as well. Today Chip is retired and Rick has his own business doing the same kind of work and so does Ron. I work in sales for Ron and his wife Becky in their company now. They have been a life saver for Sherryl and I. A wonderful provision from God.

The work that they do is very profitable and very dangerous. It has provided well financially for Sherryl's parents and her brothers, and now for us as well. It also has done so at a cost.

Sherryl's little sister Lori was a joy to all who knew her. She always was a tom boy and she had some real struggles with that part of her life. She was a good worker and worked for her dad. Lori even lived with Sherryl and I for a little while. Lori was always great with kids. Chad, Tracy and Kyley all loved her dearly.

Gerry Hall, the dear friend that had given Sherryl the Bible verse John 11:4, had befriended Lori. Gerry was like a second mother to her. Gerry helped lead Lori to the Lord and played a vital role in Lori's Christian life.

One Wednesday evening in 1988 I was bowling in the men's league with my dad and brother-in-law Roger. Someone came and told me that I had a telephone call. When I answered the phone I was given the news that Lori was dead. She had been electrocuted working on a job in Kentucky for her dad's company.

A telephone call like that is something you wish no one ever had to receive. Sherryl was found and given the news by Doug and Marta, more good friends from our church. Doug and Marta have been there for us in many difficult times. I think God's provision saw to it that they were the ones that were there to break the news to Sherryl.

In late April of 1991, Sherryl and I were sitting at our dinette table when the telephone rang again. This time Roger was on the phone calling from their vacation in Florida. At first I couldn't figure out what he was talking about. Roger assumed I knew information that I hadn't received yet. He ended up informing me that my mother was dead. Mom had suffered a massive heart attack. She died instantly as she and Dad were walking out the door of their home to go bowling. Mom was seventy seven years old and had been very healthy. Her sudden death was a shock to all of us.

My Mom and Dad were inseparable. Dad had been able to retire after I graduated from college in 1970. While they both worked at some part time jobs, just to keep busy, Mom and Dad basically had twenty one years together enjoying doing just what they wanted to do.

Without Mom, my Dad was like a fish out of water. My oldest sister Gayle moved in with Dad and helped to keep him occupied for a while. Shortly after Mom died, Sherryl, Chad and I moved in with Dad for three months while our new house was being built right across the road. Sherryl and I had purchased the lot across the street from Mom and Dad four years earlier. We looked forward to the day when we could live right across the road from them. We also liked the lot because it was only about a mile and a half from Sherryl's parent's house. We figured that we would be there so we could always help my parents in their latter years. Now, Mom was gone and Dad was just existing. He was lost without her.

It was time for another miracle! I will never forgot the way I broke the news to Dad. Dad's house was a bilevel design. When you came through the front door there were six steps up to the living room. In February of 1992 we were living with Dad and our new house was about half completed across the road. I came through the front door and Dad was leaning over the railing at the top of the stairs to greet me. "We should've built a bigger house." I said.

"What?" Dad said in that tone of voice that always told me he couldn't believe I wasn't satisfied with what we had.

"We should have built a bigger house." I repeated.

"What's wrong with your house? It looks plenty big enough to me." Dad said.

"Sherryl's going to have a baby!" I beamed.

"What?!" came his reply.

"Sherryl's—going—to—have—a—baby." I spoke slowly to him.

"You're kidding." He said. "You're not kidding?"

That was how I first announced the arrival of our next miracle.

# Chapter Sixteen

# *Meet Meghan*

✻

*I* was forty three years old, and Sherryl was thirty-nine. Chad was sixteen, Tracy and Kyley were twenty-three and nineteen years old. Needless to say, Sherryl's getting pregnant was a big surprise.

It had been ten years since I had the vasectomy reversal done. Sherryl and I had always wanted to have a baby, but the poor results I received after the reversal, plus the fact that Sherryl had one of her tubes blocked, made it seem impossible. Now, "second chance," was taking on another meaning. We were going to be given a second chance to parent a child. A chance without the difficulties that divorce causes.

Sherryl and I were excited and happy. Our church called us Abraham and Sarah. To me, it was a similar miracle to theirs. I still picture my mother up in heaven lobbying the Lord to send us a child. Not just for us, but for my Dad as well. This grandchild, living right across the road, was the medicine that made Dad's last few years without Mom bearable for him.

On August 22$^{nd}$, 1992, Meghan Leigh Perkins was born. She weighed nine pounds and thirteen ounces. She was huge! I teased Sherryl. I said she was so big, she could drive us home from the hospital! She was a big baby. Both Tracy and Kyle had weighed seven pounds. Meghan was much larger, and really plump!

Sherryl had assumed that I wanted a boy. I told her about midway through the pregnancy that I really would like a little girl. Sherryl had a son, and I thought she would like a little girl this time too. Sherryl gave me just what I ordered!

When Meghan was born, I was in the delivery room. That was my first time actually being in the room during a delivery. My two kids had been born so many years earlier, that it was before fathers were typically let into the delivery room. Sherryl had a hard time getting that little girl to finally come out of her, and into the world. When Sherryl gave that final push, Meghan literally shot out. The doctor actually had to catch her.

When babies are first born, they aren't very cute. Sherryl's mom, her sister Debbie, and her brother Ron, and his wife Becky, were all there with us. I remember how everyone would look at the baby and try to say who she looked like. Did she look more like Sherryl or me. I didn't think she looked like either of us. I thought she looked like Freddy Miller. Freddy was my plump district manager when I first started selling water treatment chemicals.

Meghan really wasn't very cute at birth. That all changed very quickly. It soon became apparent, that Meghan was going to be petite, and extremely cute. It also didn't take long to see that Meg looked very much like her mother. She has a personality like her mom as well. Nothing could have made me happier!

Sherryl was forty years old by the time Meghan was born. With all the radiation therapy and CAT scans Sherryl had, it was a great blessing that Meghan was perfectly healthy.

Sherryl and I are glad that Meghan was able to live right across the road from Grandpa Perkins. My dad had a little diversion that made being without Mom more tolerable for him. He would do all the worrying about Meghan for us. Dad would mow the lawn with Meg riding on his lap. He would baby sit her when we needed someone to stay with her. He would watch her play in the yard to be sure she didn't try to cross the road. Grandpa was good for Meghan, and Meghan was good for Grandpa.

Meghan has a way of keeping life interesting, and funny. When she was only three, I was driving her over to the baby sitter's house. We were on a back road, and I rolled through a stop sign because I could see that no one was coming. "The sign says STOP Daddy. You didn't stop?" Meghan suddenly informed me.

"I know Honey." I said. "Daddy should have stopped, but I could see that no one was coming, so I went ahead."

"The sign says STOP!" Meghan repeated to me.

"I know Honey. You're right. Daddy should've stopped. I'll be sure to stop next time." I told her.

"The sign says STOP." She said again. Then raising her hand with her thumb pointing back to the intersection we had just passed, she added, "Back up and STOP!"

That is a glimpse of Meghan. Inventive, happy, social and talented, Meghan is Sherryl all over again. She is just like that little girl who chased me around the ball field and clobbered me with her lunch box. We not only love Meghan, we like her. She is the kind of kid that is just fun to be with. Just like her mom. She makes being around her fun. I can't imagine what our lives would be like without her.

Maybe, it is because we are older, or maybe it is because we both had to share our other children's upbringing with our former spouses, but whatever the reason, Sherryl and I cherish every moment with Meghan. She is already nine years old. The time has flown by.

The other day I was driving Meghan to her soccer practice. She is in soccer, softball, basketball, and karate, as well as other activities. I was listing places she had to be that week. She looked at me, and said in all seriousness, "I've got a hard life."

I had to laugh. I said, "Meghan, don't you like doing these things. I thought they were fun for you?" Meg said, "Yes, I like doing them, but sometimes there just isn't enough time to play." Just like her mom, everyday with Meghan is an adventure. She is our gift from God.

My Dad passed away in February of 1995. When he died Meghan was two and a half years old. She was just old enough so that she can remember her Grandpa Perk.

My Dad's death was just as much of a shock as my Mother's. I was playing basketball in the church "over 35" league, when someone came in to tell me that my dad was taken to the hospital. I drove home and picked up Sherryl and Meghan and we all went to the hospital together. My Mother had died almost instantly from a massive heart attack. Dad had been healthy, so this problem was totally unexpected.

That night, at the hospital, dear friends from church stayed there with us. We were all there until about 4:00 a.m.. The doctors seemed to have Dad stabilized. It had been touch and go that evening. I remember Sherryl and me holding Dad's hand. "I want to go be with Mom." Dad said. We told him we needed him to stay with us, but he was ready to go meet the Lord and see his beloved wife again. Sherryl and I knew he wanted to go be with Mom.

The doctors told us to go home and get some rest. They thought that Dad was stable and we could come back later that morning to see him. We planned to get back to the hospital by 8 a.m., but we were so tired that we were still sleeping when the phone rang at about 9:30 in the morning. It was the hospital. Dad had just passed away.

The death of my parents was a very difficult thing for me.

They were wonderful people. They were not only my parents, they were great friends to Sherryl and me. We loved them dearly. We enjoyed their company. The one thing that made their loss bearable, was the fact that they knew the Lord. We know we will see them again. We don't know how people handle these situations without God.

My Mom had died in April of 1991. Sherryl and I moved into our new house in April of 1992. Meghan was born in August of 1992. Sherryl had a total hysterectomy in late 1993. Sherryl was still working three days a week as a registered nurse in staff development. In the summer of 1994 the first signs of trouble from Sherryl's radiation therapy began to manifest themselves. We were at Penfield Community Church for the Sunday morning service. Sherryl had an episode that resembled a tiny stroke. She started having a headache. As we sat in church, she started to have things happen with her vision. Speaking became difficult for her. She couldn't say words that she wanted to say. Because of Sherryl's background with the brain tumor, this was a very unsettling experience. We went from the church to the emergency room at her hospital.

Tests didn't show any signs of a tumor. Eventually, Sherryl's neurologist diagnosed her as having a type of migraine equivalent headache. Sherryl began having more and more trouble with her short term memory. Problems would show up where she couldn't find the word she wanted to say. When Second Chance would sing, problems with recalling lyrics happened more and more frequently. There were some changes in her personality as well. Eventually, in November of 1996, a year and nine months after my dad had died, Sherryl was dismissed from her job.

It was a severe blow to Sherryl. She had always worked. She loved her job. In some ways though, I saw it as a blessing. Sherryl became eligible for disability benefits from Social Security. This allowed her to stay home with

Meghan. Sherryl and I were both grateful for that.

Even with Sherryl not having to work at the hospital, these were busy and exciting times. Penfield Community Church had outgrown the old church building. That building had housed this historic congregation for over a hundred years. We had been having two services on Sunday mornings with Sunday School sandwiched in between. We were using two other township buildings for the children's Sunday School classes. This was bad, because it required the kids to cross a main state highway to get to their classrooms.

God was doing miracles all around us. Twenty three years before, the church had almost gone out of existence. Now, Penfield Community Church was going to build. There were those few in the congregation who mistakenly thought the church, was the old building. The church is never a building. It is the people. Those few provided some reluctance to completely leaving the old structure.

It is easy to understand sentimental attachments to a church building that holds dear memories. The old church building was the site of special memories for Sherryl and me. We were married there. My Mom and Dad had their funerals in that building. I will never forget when Pastor Tom Keller did my mother's funeral. Pastor Keller had taken over for Reverend Rugg. He invested his heart and soul into the congregation. When my Dad bent over and kissed Mom goodbye, right before we left the church to go to the cemetery, Tom broke down and wept deeply.

The building is not the church, however, the congregation is the church. In many ways, it is an indictment against any congregation when the same building can meet its needs for over a hundred years. Buildings and facilities are only tools to be used to add to the family of God. They should never be the focus of our thinking. They should never be worshipped.

I was voted to chair the building committee. We had limited resources and massive needs. There were times when the tasks we faced seemed impossible to achieve. Without God, they would never have been possible, but with Him all things are possible.

There were so many miracles that God provided so we could complete this building project. I could never list them all. He sent what seemed like a severe road block that kept us from buying land we thought we could build on. Then God provided a larger site at a better price. It was closer to the site of the original church location. When affordable financing looked like it could not be achieved, the Lord led a member to pick up a brochure on a table at the back of a church he was visiting. That led us to a company that financed church construction though bonds. This saved us thousands of dollars and made the project possible. God provided us with new members that had talents and access to equipment that saved us thousands more. Watching how road blocks kept being swept away, and the way the Lord filled our needs was a humbling experience.

The congregation learned a lot though the whole process. It was never made easy for us, but as long as we had faith to push forward, it was always made possible.

There were members on the building committee that had much more knowledge about the nuts and bolts of the project than I did. I realized that right from the beginning, and I was very grateful for their abilities and tireless work. My function was to keep us focused on the goal of meeting our most pressing need, room. We needed room enough to grow.

It was interesting to see the dynamics of how the project proceeded. I had one group of people that constantly thought we couldn't afford the size we needed the new building to be. Then there was another group of people that were always more worried about the next expansion we would face. They would worry about expanding a building we didn't even have.

I felt led to see that we had a building that would meet our

needs for at least the next 10 years. If our congregation outgrew that building, we would have the income to expand by
then. We wanted a sanctuary that would have room to seat
350 people and space for adequate Sunday School rooms.

We built a building with 13,400 square feet, for about $37
a square foot. Needless to say, it is not ornate. When we first
moved into it, in April of 1996, there was no carpeting and
only folding metal chairs to sit on. But we grew into it. Our
membership has steadily grown. So has our commitment to
the Lord.

In July of 2001 our Sunday School classrooms were
finally totally finished, and the project completely paid for.
We are nearing a point where future expansion will soon be
a reality.

In 1975 the church had no pastor, and less than 10 people
trying to keep it alive. Twenty one years later the church was
moving into a new building. God has blessed us with new
members that have wonderful testimonies. We have talented
people who are willing to use those talents for the Lord. So
many in our church have seen miracles. When people realize that God is really there, and that He knows each of us,
their lives are never the same again.

The Church is an extended family. Like any family, it has
problems. It demands commitment and effort. It is not a
social club. It is a place of worship and a center for equip-
ping the saints to take Christ to others. If your faith is personal and private, if it is not manifested in your behavior,
then what good is it? At Penfield Community Church, we
hurt when others hurt, we experience joy when others have
joy, we help when someone needs help, and we accept help
when we need it. That is what families do. We are not in
competition with other churches, we are in partnership with
every church that has Jesus as its head. Our church is far
from perfect, because it has people in it. We have our squab-
bles just like all churches do. But the Holy Spirit is there,

and He is working on us. He keeps us headed in the right direction. Sherryl and I love our extended family that is the Penfield Community Church.

I had wonderful parents. My Mom and Dad were hard-working people who were dedicated to their family. I had a wonderful childhood. The one area that my folks could have improved upon, was providing a healthy church experience during those early years. I thank God, that my parents came to know and love the Lord before they died. We were in the same church family throughout Sherryl's and my marriage. Thank God for those wonderful years.

Meghan Leigh Perkins is growing up with that church experience. The people in the church are part of her life. She has that sense of family the church provides. She accepted the Lord when she was seven years old, and was baptized at the church picnic. Sherryl and I praise God for the joy and love Meghan has brought to us. Every child is a miracle. Meghan is our very special miracle!

# Chapter Seventeen

# Trials Continue, and So Do Miracles

※

*I*t was apparent that Sherryl was going to face more trials. The long term effects from the experimental neutron radiation she received, were manifesting themselves. Sherryl was in uncharted waters. There were no survivors from that type of radiation therapy. Beginning in the summer of 1994, the problems were first diagnosed as migraine equivalent headaches. That was not what was happening. Years later, we learned that she was actually having little seizures.

Even without the headaches, Sherryl was having more and more problems with her short term memory. After she was let go from her job, there was a slow increase in deficits in her abilities.

I had left my job with Betz Laboratories. I bought a franchise mobile floor covering business, in the summer of 1990. Being in business for yourself isn't all that it's cracked up to be. By 1998, I really wanted to go back to work for somebody again. I hadn't made the best career decisions in my life. I really would have liked to remain in teaching and coaching, but that had ended twenty five years before. Now, I had a six year old little girl. Some of my high school friends, who stayed in teaching, now were nearing retirement. Here I was looking to start all over again.

I thought about entitling this book "God Takes Care of Idiots." In my case, that really applies. Through the grace of God, and the kindness of Sherryl's brother Ron and his wife Becky, I started working for their company in September of 1998. I officially closed my business for good on December 31st, 1998.

Those dates are included here to show you the perfect timing of God's provision. Sherryl had been having difficulties during the holiday season. On Monday January 4th of 1999, Sherryl had a severe headache. For the first time since the headaches she had before her tumor was discovered, she vomited from the pain. Needless to say, this was frightening for me. I arranged for Meghan to be watched, and took Sherryl to the emergency room at her former hospital. While the doctor was examining Sherryl and asking me questions about her, he looked at me, and walked over and pulled down my lower eyelid.

"I'm admitting you." The doctor said to me. He ordered a blood test to be taken on me. While he continued examining Sherryl and making arrangements for her admission to the hospital, blood was drawn from me, and tested. The results of my test came back to the doctor. He immediately said, "That can't be right. Do it again." I sat there while a second blood sample was drawn. The results came back exactly the same.

Sherryl and I were both admitted to the hospital, and placed in intensive care. I had a blood count the doctor said was "not conducive to life." That day I received four units of blood. I was extremely anemic. The doctors ordered tests to determine why. I told them what I thought the cause was. They thought it had to be something more.

The day after I was admitted, the doctor from the emergency room came up to see me. He said, "Congratulations, you were the healthiest dead guy we had all day." He explained that my blood count was lower than most people could survive. He explained that I had probably been anemic for so long, that my body had compensated to a point where I was able to survive and function, when others would be dead. He also said that bringing my wife into the emergency room the day before, may have saved my life.

I was in the hospital until Friday, January 8th. It was a terrible five days. They were days filled with unbearable pain, and boundless embarrassment. Do you want to know what almost killed me? Hemorrhoids, that's right hemorrhoids. I had suffered from them for ten years. They would bleed every couple of weeks. It was good news to learn that they were my only problem. It was sheer agony to go through the tests that made sure that nothing else was wrong.

The doctors thought that I might have colon cancer, or bleeding ulcers. I don't know what they call the test, but it is the one where fiber optic cameras go places I don't even want to think about! The preparation for this test is to drink a gallon of stuff, that makes you totally clear out your colon. I had a nurse that evening, that must have graduated from the masochist school of nursing. She had as much empathy as a great white shark. She came walking over to my bed, with a bed pan. I said, "You've got to be kidding. You want me to drink that stuff, and use a bed pan!"

She replied that the doctor's orders didn't say I could get out of bed. I said, "Lady, they don't pay you enough money to make you clean up what will happen if I have to use a bed pan!" She got the picture, and allowed me to walk over to the toilet.

Let me tell you, when you suffer from hemorrhoids like I had, the preparation for that test was a small taste of what Hell must be like. For ten hours, it was like I was sitting on a blow torch. The pain was terrible and continuous. My hemorrhoids were so enlarged and the pain was beyond belief.

I asked my nurse to give me something for the pain. "Don't you have drugs in this hospital? Morphine, heroin, laughing gas, anything! Just find me something for the pain!" I begged!

The nurse sneered at me, with an evil smile, and said that the doctor hadn't prescribed anything for me. I begged her for something. Finally, she brought me one Tylenol. One Tylenol! That was like trying to kill an elephant with a BB gun!

I didn't get any relief until I was somewhat anesthetized for the actual test procedure. The hour or so that the pain was relieved during the test, was a welcomed respite. I was in and out of consciousness during that time. When the effect of the anesthetic was wearing off, a Dr., who was a proctologist, came in to see me. He said he had to examine me. "You don't have to touch me do you?" I pleaded. He touched me! It felt like he was drilling for oil. The pain was back. At least he prescribed some pain killing medicine for me, and about an hour later, life was bearable again.

What made it even worse, was what I learned the next morning. I had a different nurse in the morning. A male, who was much more understanding. He asked me why I didn't have the shades drawn on the large windows facing the hospital parking lot.

I said, "Isn't that one way glass? People out there can't see in can they?"

"Sure they can." He said. "Especially at night, with the lights on in here."

I couldn't believe it! I have no idea why the nurse never closed the shades the night before. The windows in my room where huge. They went all the way down to within about a foot and a half of the floor. I figured that it had to be one way glass, because the nurse the night before, never acted like the shades should be drawn.

When I think about what people in that parking lot must have seen the night before, I still get embarrassed. My hemorrhoids are probably a legend in Lorain. The pain was terrible. Now the embarrassment was too. When your church family comes to visit you in the hospital and you are there because hemorrhoids almost killed you, you feel pretty stupid.

Even so, my friends from church were wonderful to me, and I appreciated their support. I was released from the hospital on Friday January 8th.

Sherryl's situation was more serious. Friday the 8th, the day I was being released, her doctors determined that Sherryl was suffering from tiny seizure episodes. They were just about to start her on seizure medication, when she suffered a grand mal seizure. This put her in a comatose state.

No one knew what to expect. When Sherryl showed no signs of responding after 36 hours, the doctors recommended we transfer her to the Cleveland Clinic. That is what we did. For the next six days there was little change. Finally, she began to come out of it. She was transferred to Metro General Hospital in Cleveland and placed in their rehabilitation program.

It was a long slow process, but Sherryl made steady progress. For the next three months she remained in the hospital. She went through physical, occupational and speech therapy. Finally, she was able to come home.

During these past few years, especially since my parents have been gone, Sherryl's mom and dad have been wonderful to us. They have helped us in so many ways. We love them dearly. We play cards with them at least once a week. It is good therapy for Sherryl, and she really enjoys it.

A card game with Sherryl's folks is a real trip. Her mother has the worst poker face in the history of card playing. She makes more faces than Lon Channey. She is also the worst table talker you ever saw. She is always giving her partner little hints as to what she has in her hand. I always kid her. I tell her that her mansion in heaven will be a pot-a-potty, because she is such a cheater at cards. Sherryl's father has his little tricks too. He does more than his fair share table talking as well. Sherryl's dad lays his card on the table in such a way, as to tell her mom, when he has the next winning card a certain suit. Sherryl's mom is so focused on her cards, that she never gets his signal to her anyway. Our card games would make a purest ill. That is why we all get a bang out of them.

Sherryl's parents have made the last couple of years so much easier for us to bear. We are glad that they know the Lord and have been there for us.

Sherryl hasn't been allowed to drive since the grand mal seizure in January of 1999. This is the biggest thing that bothers her. She was always on the go. Not being able to drive frustrates her more than anything. Her mom and dad have been there to help take Sherryl and Meghan places when I can't. Her sister Debbie has also been a big help and support for us. Debbie is like Meghan's second mom. Sherryl's brother Ron, and wife Becky have provided me with a job. The position I have in their company, has given me the flexibility to cope with our current situation better than any other job ever could.

Sherryl and I have truly been blessed with wonderful families. Every member of both her and my family have always been there for us. Our church family has been as well. We are humbled, by all the wonderful people around us.

The past three years have not been easy. Sherryl has been back in the hospital two more times. Each time she had to go through short periods of rehab again. Each time she has bounced back. The last time she was in the hospital was in December of 2000. She had bleeding that occurred in her brain. The bleeding caused a hematoma that made Sherryl sick when she moved. It also caused her speech to slow and slur. The hematoma also affected her peripheral vision in her left eye. The bleeding had stopped and there was nothing we could do but wait for the hematoma to clear up. She was in the hospital about two weeks and went through rehab again.

At our request, her doctor at Metro General changed her seizure medication. The medicine she had been using, made her very tired and very hungry. It caused her to gain over thirty pounds. The original radiation had harmed her thyroid gland and was a factor in some weight gain she had after her surgery. Sherryl had been such an active healthy person, but the physical problems she's had led to changes in her life, that she couldn't help.

The change in seizure medication has helped. Since the beginning of 2001, Sherryl has lost over forty five pounds. She has been doing the best she has since January of 1999. She has started to sing again with me, and with Second Chance, on a limited basis.

Even so, for Sherryl and I, it is a roller coaster ride. As I write this chapter, she is having trouble with her vision and speech again. I have been told that episodes like the one caused by the hematoma she had, may occur at any time.

Other than my salvation, Sherryl is the most wonderful gift God has ever given me. The Lord does take care of idiots. When we first met, she was a beautiful woman, smart, independent, energetic, giving, athletic, take charge, and every other great thing a man could want in a wife and friend. Through no fault of Sherryl's, many things have changed for her. Those changes have made things more difficult for both of us.

Sherryl's eyesight has been very negatively affected. She has significant hearing loss. She sometimes gets confused and goes the wrong way in our own house. Her speech and movement is often slowed considerably. Her memory problems and physical problems can be very frustrating for both of us. With all those changes, she is still God's greatest blessing to me. I love her more every day. I respect her more every day. I miss what Sherryl was like, but I love and praise God for what she is like. Every day with Sherryl, is a blessing from God.

I guess that brings me to the point of this book.

God is God. I'm not. If I was God, I would restore Sherryl to complete health. I ask Him for that every day. So does Sherryl. Up until now, that hasn't happened. I don't know why. Maybe it is because I still need to learn some things. Maybe Sherryl has to learn some things. We don't know the reason.

Do I get impatient with God? Yes I do. Sometimes, I get angry, because I haven't gotten my own way yet. Sherryl is my mate. I love her with all my heart. I hate to see her have any problems. Realistically, it is not all my concern for her. I selfishly want the companion I married, my very best friend!

There are times when I get frustrated with Sherryl, and with God. There are times when I treat Sherryl poorly, for things that she can't help. Recently, Sherryl had her thirtieth class reunion. One of the guys in her class said that I was the best thing that ever happened to Sherryl, because I was standing by her. I told him that he had it wrong. Sherryl is the best thing that ever happened to me.

Sherryl and I are eternally grateful for all the miracles that God has done in our lives. God actually spoke to me and kept me from suicide. God brought us together and filled our lives with love after failed marriages. The Lord allowed us to sing and testify to His love and mercy. He put us in a church family that accepted us and has allowed us to serve and be served for the past twenty years. The Lord saved Sherryl from the deadliest form of brain cancer. He gave us a daughter that has been the joy of our lives. God provided me with a job that has allowed us the time and freedom to cope with the past two years. He even used Sherryl's seizures to get me to medical attention that probably saved my life.

Those are just a few of the miracles God has done for us. Yet we continue to ask Him for more.

The one thing I want the readers of this book to understand is this. God is real. He knows you and He loves you. He loves you more than you can comprehend. We may not get everything we want. He doesn't answer every prayer with the answer we think is best. He does answer every prayer with the answer that is best. His ways are higher than our ways. He will accomplish His purpose.

I pray that Sherryl will be allowed to live with me and serve the Lord until the day He raptures His Bride, the Church, out of this world. I pray that "Second Chance" will be able to sing and minister again. That we may help people join God's family. I pray that Meghan will have her mom with her, vital and full of life. Making her do her homework, reminding her to brush her teeth, and doing all the other things loving moms do.

Whatever happens, Sherryl and I thank God for the adventure He has given us. We claim His word, John 11:4, "This sickness will not end in death. No, it is for God's glory so that God's Son may be glorified through it." We believe that God's Son has already been glorified through the miracles he has given us. We thank Him for all He has done for us.

The natural man thinks we are crazy to ask God to restore damaged brain tissue. The natural man does not know God. If the Lord can restore the brain of Lazarus after he had been dead four days, then restoring a brain with some radiation damage is no problem.

Sherryl and I want God to restore her. We both know that the Lord can restore her, if that is what he chooses to do.

Should Sherryl be renewed, we will do all we can to let people know about the God we love and serve. We have no doubts that God can do it, our faith knows that.

We also know, that our faith is not what heals. God heals. We don't have faith in our faith, we have faith in God. We are not God, He is. God is not our servant or personal genie. No matter what our future holds, we will always love and praise the Lord. With all the Lord has done for us, we would be crazy if we didn't.

*The End*

Printed in the United States
745300003B